Flying High in Spirit

Also by Roberta Grimes

The Fun of Dying
The Fun of Staying in Touch
The Fun of Growing Forever
Liberating Jesus
My Thomas

Flying High in Spirit

A young Snowboarder's Account of His Ride Through Heaven

By
Mikey Morgan
as told to Carol Morgan
with Roberta Grimes

Flying High in Spirit
by: Mikey Morgan as told to Carol Morgan with Roberta Grimes

Publisher's Cataloging-In-Publication Data
(Prepared by The Donohue Group, Inc.)
Names: Morgan, Mikey, 1987-2007 (Spirit) | Grimes, Roberta.
Title: Flying high in spirit : a young snowboarder's account of his ride through heaven / by Mikey Morgan, with: Roberta Grimes.
Description: Madison, VA : Christine F. Anderson Publishing & Media, [2015] | Interest age level: 13 and up.
Identifiers: ISBN 978-0-692-54435-8 | ISBN 978-0-692-26424-9 (ebook)
Subjects: LCSH: Morgan, Mikey, 1987-2007 (Spirit) | Future life. | Spiritualism. | Snowboarders--Colorado. | Truth. | Spirit writings.
Classification: LCC BF1301 .M67 2015 (print) | LCC BF1301 (ebook) | DDC 133.93--dc23

Published by
Christine F. Anderson Publishing & Media, Madison VA, 22727
www.cfapublishing.com

CHRISTINE F. ANDERSON

Cover Design by David Cahn

ISBN: 978-0692544358

Printed in the United States of America

Purpose and Dedication

I am thrilled to have reconnected with my mom so she and I could write this book! My dream is to give hope and peace and a better life to everyone on earth.

I want you to know that we are not far away when we transition back to heaven. Our loving connections never end! Communication is possible between dimensions. Death on earth is only a temporary physical separation. We hear you, see you, and guide you along the journey of life on earth. We show up for your important events, and we enjoy being a part of them. We still care about you and love you very much! You will see us and be reunited with us. And a hug in heaven is a hundred times better that a hug on earth. I promise you that!

Love is the key to everything.

I would like to thank Roberta Grimes for believing in my mother's communication ability and giving her the opportunity to share the knowledge that I am giving to her. This book could not have happened without the amazing skills of Roberta Grimes! She has become a very dear friend of mine.

This book is dedicated to my many loved ones on earth, especially my parents and my brother, Joey. I want to specifically acknowledge my friends from Colorado at CSU who were with me when I transitioned back home. Please understand that this was a plan that was being fulfilled. We couldn't have prevented it. I would not have wanted to try to prevent it.

The knowledge and love brought forth through my communications with my mom are meant to give you hope, peace, and comfort for many years to come. Please remember me, and remember the message in the song "Love Generation!" BELIEVE!

—Mikey Morgan, a/k/a DJ "Mikey Mo"

TABLE OF CONTENTS

FOREWORD
BY ROBERTA GRIMES

I have spent my life studying afterlife communications and relevant aspects of quantum mechanics and other scientific disciplines, and at length I have assembled a fairly complete picture of what happens at and after death. I have avoided altogether reading anything channeled after 1950. I have avoided even talking with people who claimed they could channel information from the dead, for fear that the wonderfully detailed and consistent picture that I had assembled over decades might be corrupted by some deluded writer's ravings.

Then in the spring of 2011 I met Carol Morgan. Her older son had died three years before. Carol had learned to communicate with Mikey by pendulum, which is an ancient method of spirit communication in which at the time I did not believe. Her telling me that Mikey was claiming to be a sixth-level being made me cringe. The dead consistently describe about seven levels of post-death reality, the sixth of which is inhabited by beings who are so well-developed spiritually that they are close to rejoining the Source. Sixth-level beings have no need to incarnate. Communications purported to come from them usually are stilted pronouncements that can sound inexplicable to people on earth.

My journey from comforting a mother in grief to making friends with an elevated being was a long one. When Carol demonstrated her communication method to me, this tentative waif of a grieving mother was transformed in ways that made me confident that at least she believed in what she was doing. She would immediately be laughing and chatting as her pendulum merrily swung. Nobody is that good an actress.

So I invited Carol to join afterlifeforums.com, a website where knowledgeable members help visitors answer afterlife-related questions. Carol began to ask Mikey to answer questions that people were posting on the website, always following her answers with, "That's one opinion, anyway," or, "That's what Mikey says," or even, "I don't know if this is right." She told me at the time that she found a lot of what Mikey was telling her to be unbelievable. And I was reading every response as she posted it, always ready to correct her mistakes.

But there were no mistakes. None! After a half-century of study, I have as much evidence-based knowledge of death and the period after death as do the earth's best experts. There are few people with whom I even can discuss the more esoteric details. But incredibly, within weeks I knew that I could add Mikey Morgan to the very short list of genuine afterlife experts.

Carol Morgan began her journey knowing nothing about this field. Her interest in it had tragically begun when Mikey had died at the age of twenty. Yet over that next year, I watched as Mikey through Carol answered hundreds of afterlife-related questions, often in extensive detail, including mentions of things that no one other than a few top experts could have known. Soon I was noticing that he even would occasionally go a step beyond what I had put together and fill in little consistent details. It became obvious to me that Carol Morgan was channeling a very advanced being.

Soon afterlifeforums.com had established a thread where only Mikey answered questions. By now, that thread has thousands of posts. And never in all those answers has Mikey deviated, even slightly, from what I know to be true based upon my study of nearly two centuries worth of evidence. Never have I had to correct a word. At this point, I have no doubt that Mikey Morgan is a sixth-level being who chose to live an optional brief earth-life so he would be able to teach through the veil in the language of a modern twenty-year-old.

To better understand what Mikey has to tell us, you should know that approximately seven afterlife levels of reality exist right where we are, but at higher vibratory frequencies, just as the channels of your TV set range from lower to higher frequencies. Right now, your mind is tuned to your own particular body on what we believe is the lowest level of reality. When you die, your mind will tune to a higher level as easily as you change TV channels, and there it will pick up a whole new solid reality. Each of the seven primary afterlife levels is enormous, perhaps as large as the entire universe. In addition, each of the levels has many gradations within it, so there are infinite beautiful and solid places to which your mind might tune at death.

Our minds are able to be comfortable at higher and higher vibratory levels as we become better developed spiritually. We can't go higher than the level to which our degree of spiritual development suits us, but we always can lower our spiritual vibratory rate. So even though our loved ones on earth are at a lower vibratory level than we are, we can return to their level and communicate with them. We can attend family reunions on Level Three, which is the lowest of the beautiful Summerland levels and seems to be where most people enter the afterlife, and also where families congregate. We easily can go lower. And as we become more developed spiritually, it is possible for us to go much higher.

The highest of the solid-seeming afterlife levels is Level Six. Those who have attained the sixth level can travel by mind anywhere in the afterlife levels except to Level Seven, which is the Celestial level, what we believe to be the vibratory center of God. I used to accept the general view that entering Level Seven meant rejoining and merging with the Source in a one-way trip called the "second death," but apparently I was wrong about that. Mikey has helped me see that I have been wrong about a number of things. For another example, since nearly all communications from the dead come from people on the middle afterlife levels who don't know much about what is above them, I long had thought that the top two levels were largely or entirely non-material. So I have been delighted to make a friend in Mikey! He actually lives on the sixth level, and he is happy to poke around and answer questions.

Mikey's story and his perspective are unique. Wearing the persona of his recent earth-lifetime as easily as he still wears his baseball cap, he speaks as a boy just becoming a man in words that make sense to us today. Yet as a being who often dons spirit robes and frequents the universities that he assures us are abundant on Level Six, he can tell us as few communicators in history have been able to tell us how we can best use our lives to make spiritual progress. Mikey chose to enter a new earth-body nearly four centuries after he had ceased to incarnate because he wanted to re-familiarize himself with earth-life so he could share with us what we so badly need to learn. He is joyous to find you willing to listen!

Chapter One
I Died and Went to Heaven

At the beginning of my junior year at Colorado State University, some friends and I took a weekend camping trip into the Rocky Mountains. On that afternoon, there were five of us in a truck that was one of several on a mountain trail where we could enjoy the amazing scenery. We were chillin'. Havin' fun. Not a worry in the world.

I was in the midst of the best time of my life. Going to college at CSU in Colorado and working as a DJ at the most popular restaurant and club near campus was so sweet! Whenever I had a free moment, I was hitting the mountains for some serious snowboarding. Copper Mountain was my favorite place to ride. Beautiful! Love that powder. I was livin' the dream and takin' it all in.

Choosing just the right songs to play as the DJ at Washington's on the nights when I worked was very important to me. I worked hard to be the main DJ on the big college nights. Song choice was critical, and I had my favorites. Wearing my Minnesota Twins baseball cap had long been my tradition and style.

Twice during my college years I had gone to Mexico on spring breaks, and while there I had heard the most awesome song ever! It was "Love Generation" by Bob Sinclar. He sings another song called "World Hold On" which is pretty sweet, too. Both songs talk about love, peace, and unity. Really what life is all about. I love the messages that songs can give. I would play those songs every chance I got, especially "Love Generation." It had become my trademark.

I had only days before been telling my boss that my life couldn't get any better. Living so close to the mountains and playing songs for all the college kids was incredibly awesome. The best! And taking time out with family and friends and going to the mountains was what I really loved. Playing John Denver's "Rocky Mountain High" sure set the mood when I was with my family, but I never let my college buddies know that I was such a John Denver fan!

So some of my buddies and I were taking a drive through the mountains early on that September evening, not a care in the world, looking forward to another great college year. With no warning, our truck rolled off the trail and down a hill. Right before the impact, I shot out of my body. Then my physical body was ejected from the truck through the sunroof, which had shattered. It was crazy! I could see the damaged truck from above, and there I was, lying near it on the ground.

What the heck was happening? Was this a dream? It felt too real to be a dream! I knew I was fine. I felt no discomfort of any kind, which didn't make sense, when it was obvious that my body down there wasn't doing well. Panic and fear set in with my friends as they got out of the truck. What was going on? I didn't understand it, and that started to scare me.

That was when I noticed that something was changing with me. I felt different. I was weightless, light, and free-flowing. I was actually in the air, just above that scene and watching everything. It didn't make sense with what I had just been doing with my buddies, trail riding and enjoying our weekend. I was feeling this crazy sensation that was intense! It is hard to explain, but I was becoming dynamic with my energy, with my thoughts and feelings. Crazy tingling! Really a total head rush. I felt like I was everywhere! It was so easy to move. Literally took no effort. I could feel my friends' emotions, so I knew that their fear was intense and building. There was nothing I could do to stop it.

As I was focused on them below me, I realized that there were people appearing in the air around me. They were greeting me, loving me, and I was recognizing them and realizing that I knew them well, but I hadn't seen them in awhile. What the heck were they doing here? I was remembering now having done so much with them, shared so much, but not recently. They also were moving without effort, floating . . . .

I gradually began to feel intense and radiant love. But where was it coming from? I felt a tug away from everything that I knew. It was an energy force that was guiding me, almost pushing me, but I was OK with that. As I turned and looked back, I felt concerned for my friends on earth as they struggled to save me. I wanted to help them! But I was already saved. I was just fine. Why couldn't they see that? This was what was so confusing to me. I felt great, but I was obviously having problems by how my friends were reacting.

At the same time, I felt I was beginning to go to a different place with the guidance of these kind and loving people. They told me not to worry. Everything was all right. There was a definite energy pull now. I was being drawn to something different. No other way to describe it. It had a very comfortable feeling because of the love that accompanied it. There was light, too. A warm and comforting light embraced me that was different from anything I ever had felt on earth. It was pretty intense! I realized at this point that I must be in two different places at once. Not sure how that could happen, but that was how it felt to me. I could still see what was happening on earth, but it was gradually becoming more faint and transparent. The place I was being guided or pulled to was becoming very real and solid. The process of what I was experiencing was coming back to me. I felt like I may have done this before.

* * *

As we moved, I realized that I no longer heard what was going on at the accident scene. I was coming into a place that was incredibly beautiful and peaceful. I had no fear or worry. It felt like home. My loving companions looked at me and told me I was back in heaven.

What?! Heaven? Are you kidding me?

They continued to speak to me in ways that I would understand, giving me only comforting information in an attempt to get me to comprehend what was going on. I couldn't help but become excited as I looked around. The music I heard was incredible, melodies beyond anything I could have imagined. The scenery of nature was alive with magnificent color and texture. Brilliant in every sense of the word! There were beautiful buildings and amazing statues, rich with incredible detail and brilliant color. Some of these works of art around me were portrayals of life events on earth, and one that I noticed symbolized the unveiling of a memorial to honor loved ones who had worked hard to create positive influences for the betterment of other people. I recalled without anyone's having to say it that there are people here in heaven who take careful notice of the good that folks are doing on earth, and they memorialize it in beautiful works of art. The love and warm light that surrounded everything was incredibly comforting.

Everyone I saw around me was so happy! I could tell they were doing things they enjoyed. And what was really interesting was how they moved about. Some were walking, some were in vehicles, and some were simply floating by. The vehicles were amazing! Some looked like cars, some like little spaceships or planes, and some like bikes. How ever they were moving, it looked smooth and effortless. I noticed no exhaust or smoke. It really was magical to watch! People only had to think about how they wanted to move, and it happened. There seemed to be a kind of hidden energy that propelled all these people and their vehicles, if they chose to use vehicles. Some people looked like they were actually flying, yet some could simply move instantaneously. It was crazy!

Someone said that I was back in the Summerlands, the middle dimensions of heaven.

"Whatever that is," was my thought. It was incredibly impressive.

As I stood there, looking around, people were starting to approach me and welcome me home. The hugs I received were like no others; they were filled with incredible love and comfort that empowered me. The joyous reunions with so many loved ones were tremendous! But I needed a moment to adjust and gather my thoughts of what had just happened. I needed to get a grip on this. What I had experienced obviously was not a dream. "I was just in Colorado, having a great time in the mountains with my college buddies, and now I am here, in heaven? Really? A totally different place that feels just as solid and real as earth? Doesn't seem to be possible!"

Yet all of this was gradually coming back to me as I felt the comfort and love that permeated the place. I pulled myself together as I was taking it all in, checking things out. Then my loving companions told me I needed to continue on to the Sixth Plane or aspect of heaven. As I followed them, which was just a matter of changing the feeling or essence of my being, an intense sensation came over me. It is hard to explain, but I felt more alive than ever! The feeling of strong, sincere love was everywhere. I was comfortable beyond anything I could ever remember. I had so much energy within me, I felt I could explode with excitement!

* * *

Moving to a higher aspect was simply a matter of increasing the energy vibration of my being. As we arrived in the sixth aspect of heaven, I was overwhelmed by the more intense beauty all around me. There were several majestic university buildings together, looking surprisingly earthlike, made of brick and stone and even some of them in wood, but the difference was that they all looked pristine. Not a bit of peeling paint or wear to be seen! And the architecture was spectacular, including steeples that went up high into the sky. Unbelievable! There was artwork, much of it lovely paintings of people who had accomplished wonderful things. The scenery was lush and richly colored, the greenery far more abundant and beautiful than earth's vegetation. The flowers were intensely bright, some in colors never seen on earth, and they actually turned their faces to me as I moved among them. There were kinds of trees that I never had seen, some with flowers on them. And they never dropped a petal.

Besides the university buildings, there were dwellings of various sizes and descriptions, around which I saw people relaxing and enjoying one another's company. No two were exactly alike. Some looked like earth homes, while others had sharp angles with unusually-shaped windows and doors and random openings. What struck me most was that everything was in such perfect condition! It was all far more beautiful, more elegant, and in every way richer than anything I had experienced on earth.

There were people busy around me. A lot seemed to be going on, and I could not help but notice all the teaching that was going on throughout that beautiful university. There were people who appeared as scholars or teachers dressed in robes of different colors. As things began to come back to me, I sat down on a bench outside one of the buildings of the university with my guides nearby, and I collected my thoughts. My vision was amazing! I could see everywhere around me, and even behind me. Wow! This was where I was to reside, and I could feel the true comfort of being at home rising in me. I felt tremendous peace. At this point, full knowledge came over me from all of my experiences from before and during my recent life on earth.

I became one with this knowledge, and one with the true essence of my spiritual being.

That was when I realized that I had just merged with my Higher Self. Now I understood what I was experiencing, and the plan that was being fulfilled. My time on earth was complete. I understood now that four of these friends who had helped guide me here from that accident scene were actually my spirit guides. They had watched over me during my time on earth, trying to keep me on track. Prior to my coming to earth this last time, I had worked with these awesome individuals who actually were close eternal friends, and in their intense love and support of me, they had agreed to take on the responsibility of being my guides.

* * *

Soon after my arrival on the sixth level of heaven, my eternal home, I met with my three Higher Guides for my life review. These Guides are very advanced and knowledgeable beings who have achieved the upper aspects of the sixth level; I call them my "Elders." We have been together for a very long time, through many experiences. Everyone has guides, although some change from time to time, depending upon our mission and what we hope to accomplish. I am mid-sixth-level in my development. At my stage, most of those guiding us are from the upper aspects of Level Six, very near the Source level.

My Elders sat down with me in a big conference hall around a table. We all reviewed my life plan together. This particular conference hall was in a beautiful and stately building that looked as if it were made of brick, artfully done and of course looking brand-new. My last earth-lifetime necessary for me to grow spiritually had been lived in the 1600s, so this sitting for a life review was familiar, but at the same time foreign. I had managed a great deal of spiritual development since that last, long-ago life review.

My life review this time around seemed to take perhaps four hours as you would reckon earth-time. We went over all the pertinent aspects of my life just completed. It was like watching a movie in front of me, with my thoughts giving images of the many aspects of my short life. I discussed the things that had happened in my earthly life from my perspective, getting feedback from my Elders along the way. Overall, they were proud of me, and praised what I had accomplished in such a short time.

I should stress here that during our life reviews, it is the intention of our actions that is most important! We didn't go over every petty thing that had no bearing on my spiritual needs, like all the ridiculous parking tickets I got on campus. That was irrelevant to how I interacted with others. As we focused on my interactions with other people, I could feel not only my own emotions, but also the emotions of those around me in the movie of my life. Moments of sadness and moments of joy. I was reminded, and I well understood, that the only person we can control is our self. As my life review went on, I came to think that I had done the best that I could have done, especially considering how young I had been. I had always tried to be a nice kid. It had felt so good to be loved by others, and I had wanted very much to please them. I had had a wonderful relationship with my parents and brother, with minimal difficulties at any point in my whole earth-lifetime. Becoming adult does give us more opportunity to experience various relationships and to improve our ability to deal with others, and I hadn't had much opportunity for that this time around.

My perspective here was so different! I recalled that while I was on earth, I had struggled with individuals who were homosexual. I had tried to avoid having anything to do with them. After returning to heaven, I could now understand that these individuals were no different than I was, and I never should have judged them. I was reminded to understand that no one ever is perfect while in human form. Greater understanding comes through all our experiences, even including my present one, which required that I leave the earth dimension at a young age so I could work on teaching about the importance of love and the afterlife through the veil with my mom, who is still on earth. This whole life-review experience felt like watching a movie of my life and having it critiqued by my teachers. Pretty crazy! I wasn't perfect with everything, but I had given it my best shot, and I was pleased with that. I had tried hard to deliver the message of love, peace, and unity in a way that was acceptable to my age group. I also had had a very close relationship with my immediate family, who were the ones with whom I now needed to reconnect so we could continue our plan of teaching through the veil.

* * *

As I was finishing my life review, I was suddenly overwhelmed as I felt the strong emotions of my family and friends on earth. Because of my loving connection with them, these channels were wide open! The sadness and intense grief I was feeling became overwhelming. I needed to go and help them, and now. My Elders could see that I was becoming emotional. They understood that I needed to leave.

I quickly moved by changing the vibration of my being, drawing close again to the earth dimension. I thought of where I wanted to go, and I was there in an instant! It was amazing how I could move. I had forgotten how easy it is to get around when you are free of an earthly body. I also realized that heaven is not far away from the earth. To tell you the truth, it's actually in the same place! The process of getting to heaven is a matter of changing our vibrational frequency within our being of who we really are. I realized quickly that the earth dimension has a lower vibration to it than heaven. When we transition and leave our earthly body, it is the increase in our vibration of our true being, our consciousness, that makes us progress onward to our true home. We are energy!

As I drew close to the earth dimension, the first place I went was to the living room of my family's home in Minnesota, where my parents were hearing the news of the accident from a policeman. It was 4:30 in the morning. A paramedic and a minister were there also. They told my parents that their son Mikey had been killed in an SUV roll-over accident in the mountains of Colorado the previous evening. My heart absolutely ached, watching them and their reaction. Reality hit me hard! I began to cry as my emotions got the best of me.

What was also very troubling to me was that the story the policeman was telling them about the accident was wrong. The details were incorrect. Maybe it shouldn't have mattered as much as it did, but it was so important to me that my parents not judge or blame my friends. I followed my parents as they woke up my little brother to tell him what had happened to me. Watching them all was so painful. I just felt horrible! The emotions of my family were so intense, but they placed no blame on anyone. They desperately wanted to comfort my friends who had been with me when I had passed. When my parents called the coroner, they were told not to come to Colorado because there was nothing they could do. The coroner told my parents that he would be sending me back to Minnesota when all legalities were met to allow my body to be flown back home.

My heart ached for them. I love my family so much! I wished they didn't have to go through this, but it had been my time to leave. I just wished so badly that they could see me. I was still very much alive. They needed to know this!

Chapter Two
Proving My Survival

As the news quickly spread, many relatives and friends came to my family's home to give them support. My family was getting calls from all over the United States as loved ones found out what had happened to me. I was going all over the place, trying to help. I could move at the blink of an eye. Many loved ones were talking out loud to me, crying, and praying. I could hear and see them clearly. One family friend, Bob, who called early on when he heard the news, told my mom to pay attention to signs from me. Bob said they will come "fast and furious," and she should write them down. He said, "Mikey is going to let you know that he's fine!" Bob had received many signs from his wife when she had passed a few years before. My parents were very interested in these stories. Even then, they knew that signs were possible.

I was desperate to initiate communication, and fast! I knew I had the ability to make things happen in the earthly dimension by my energy and the way that my true being vibrated. I began to manipulate things, trying to let everyone know how close I was.

It's important that you understand both how difficult it is for us spiritual beings to communicate with you, and how we make it happen. To do anything on the earth plane, I have to draw my vibration down as close as I can to yours on earth. I am definitely concentrating on what I am doing through this whole process. It is all done by my mind's energy. The fact that we spiritual beings are in a timeless dimension and you on earth are not gives us the ability to make things happen at exactly the right moment to get your attention.

I can put thoughts into someone's head telepathically, and give someone the idea to turn on a radio at a specific time or change the station to get the song I'm after. I also might distract someone so they leave for the store a little later, and the song that I want them to hear will be playing when they walk in. Understand that we spiritual beings know what music is coming up in the store, as well as the radio station that you on earth often listen to, especially if we have a loving connection. I can put a thought into your head to remind you of me just as the song begins. Working with radios, iPods, CD players, or PA frequencies is easy because when I change my own frequency or how I vibrate even slightly, I can affect what is being played. For this to occur, I draw very close to the electrical aspect of the device that is delivering the music. When a battery is being used to supply energy to the device, I use my own energy to interrupt the energy flow, which can alter what is being played. It's similar to what you might do to push a button on a CD player to change from song to song.

We even can put thoughts of something we want to say to you telepathically into the mind of someone else, and that includes a DJ on the radio or a complete stranger! I am familiar with certain playlists, some from when I was still on earth, and I learn new ones simply by scanning the device with my mind. I will literally go to the radio station. Sometimes more than one spiritual being will work together to get a needed job done. Our thoughts travel in an instant, and we can move immediately just by thinking. I know that sounds crazy, but it's true. Remember that we communicate telepathically. And all our minds are very powerful.

I found that I was almost immediately able to give my family clues to my survival. I soon discovered that focusing on electronics worked especially well for me. People were gathering at our house to support my family as they heard the news about the accident. I started right in with the radio as soon as our neighbor friend, Dorene, turned it on in our family's home on that following morning. I manipulated frequencies and playlists to have John Denver be the first singer everyone heard.

* * *

For years I had worn a Minnesota Twins baseball cap. It was rare to see me without it on. I had received a new cap that year for my birthday from my Aunt Jean, but I hadn't thrown out my old worn one. As I drew close to the earthly dimension by changing my vibration, I heard my mom talking on the phone to my friend from Colorado about how badly she wanted my baseball cap. That cap was so important to her! My mom wanted my buddies from Colorado to send her my cap and some of my clothes for the funeral.

When my two Minnesota Twins baseball caps were delivered separately to my family's home during the week after I died, I manipulated the CD player to have the song "My Sweet Lady" by John Denver playing for my mom each time one of them arrived. While she listened to the song lyrics, I felt great, watching her reaction. I knew that she was feeling my presence. She truly believed and knew it was me talking to her! And that was just what I was doing, through the music. What gave her such validation that it had to be me was that it happened not once, but twice! The message this song gave her was critical in view of what was about to unfold. She replayed that song for several people who stopped by the house, telling them she was sure the song had played because of me!

Getting certain songs to play on the CD player when it was on was easy to influence with my energy. I was close enough to it to see what CDs were on my parents' device, and I knew the John Denver CD very well, including the order of the songs. I am not pushing buttons on the CD player, but instead I'm using my mind's energy to get a certain song to play by changing frequencies within the device. I could get a message across to them with the lyrics of music with careful timing, as I was now in a timeless dimension.

On earth, time gives order and sequence to events as they occur. There is a before, now, and after period with everything that you do. In heaven, there is no time and there are no restraints that go with time. We never run out of time to get something completed. Everything that we spiritual beings do is in the present. Therefore, everything for us in the heavenly dimensions is in the "now" category for time. While you are experiencing the "before" time period, I have a moment to get ready with what I want to plug into your "now" time frame in regards to a sign. I can see and hear what you are planning to do, which gives me time as it is measured on your level in which I can set up my message or give you a song as I manipulate things with my energy.

I continued to follow my family members and friends around, trying to get their attention. Once I found my dad crying on our front steps. I hated seeing that. I felt so helpless! In desperation, I moved the flag on our flagpole as though it was flapping in the wind even though there was no wind, just hoping to get his attention. He looked up and saw it, and that sign from me turned out to be very significant for him. As our loved ones talked about me in the kitchen of our home, I interrupted the electric current flowing to the ceiling fan light with my energy to get the lights to flicker on and off. Now, that certainly got their attention! I think it startled a few of them. I still love to do this type of sign!

Then I took on those vacuum cleaners. My family knew how much I hated the sound of a vacuum cleaner. During the week between my passing and the funeral, my family had many visitors coming and going to give then help and support. My Aunt Jean decided to do some cleaning while she was there, and she began to vacuum the upstairs of our house. This was when I started having some fun! As she worked, all seemed to be going well, but as soon as she got to the doorway of my bedroom, I burned that vacuum out. Smoke and all! I simply gave it a surge of my energy that was more than it could handle. Perfect timing! My mom asked what the smell was, and my aunt told her what had happened right at my doorway.

Both my mom and dad said, "Mikey always hated the sound of a vacuum!"

My mom then called a neighbor to borrow their vacuum to finish cleaning the main level. My Uncle Dale took the neighbor's vacuum and started to clean on the main floor, and I did it again. The vacuum began to smell and smoke.

My mom, who was nearby, said out loud, "Mikey, don't burn out this vacuum! It isn't mine. And we need to get the house cleaned up."

I backed off with my energy then, and the vacuum worked perfectly the rest of the time. Watching my relatives laugh about this during such a difficult time was a comfort to me. To erase all doubt that I had been the one who had been messing with their vacuum cleaners, I checked in on my grandmother at her house that was some distance away, and I burned out her vacuum cleaner, too, that same day.

* * *

I was working almost constantly to make sure they knew that I was right there with them. A few days after my passing, my brother and my cousin Sadie were sitting upstairs at home when they decided to call me on my cell phone. They listened to my voice on my voicemail. It was about 11:00 PM. Within a minute after they called, I made our house phone ring by using my energy in a manner that was specific to this device.

My way of doing this differs from what I said above, since I'm working with the sound capability of the phone. It's very important to have it ring! And I need it to seem that an actual call is coming in, so when the phone is picked up there won't be a dial tone. I simply think of making a call, which causes my energy to simulate an actual call coming through the line. This causes the phone to ring. We spiritual beings in the afterlife do this more than you folks on earth may realize with landline phones. How often do you get a call and pick it up and the phone is just silent? You may think it's a telemarketer, but it may not be! When there is absolute silence, no background noise, it may actually be a call from us in heaven.

In this case, I made the phone ring and my dad picked up the receiver to answer it. Joey and Sadie walked down from upstairs and heard my dad saying, "Hello, is anybody there? Hello . . . ?" Dad looked at them and said, "No one is on the line!"

Joey and Sadie looked at each other, and then looked at our dad and said, "We just called Mikey's cell phone a minute ago. That must have been him calling us back."

I was thrilled to have accomplished this! And what I loved was that my brother and cousin had realized that it was me.

* * *

When several of my friends came from Colorado for the funeral, I knew that I had work to do. Our house was now full of people, so I needed to create a sign of great impact. It was a beautiful fall day with a lot of sunshine. I rounded up a number of loving beings and spirit guides from the afterlife realms to help with my efforts. Together, we have much greater ability than any of us would have alone, and we can achieve profound things within the dimensions, which are different energy frequencies literally overlapping in the same place. Together, our combined energies or frequencies can create amazing things! The more advanced we are, the more we can accomplish. Remember that everything is energy-based.

Together, my eternal friends and I were powerful. Using our combined energies, we produced a brief cloud and rain shower that had some fabulous wind to it, which quickly passed over our house. Having that moisture in the air gave us the tool to create a perfect and brilliant double rainbow just outside the house that was very impressive. My cousin, Connor, who was outside playing at the time, came running in to tell everyone what he was seeing. When many friends and family walked out the door of our house to see it, I forced three geese (literally pushed them with my energy) to fly low over everyone's heads through the center of the rainbow to really get their attention. Holy cow, did that get a reaction! And what was really cool was listening to the TV weatherman on the evening news. He said, "What a beautiful day we had in the Twin Cities with all the magnificent sunshine. The only issue was the brief rainstorm that truly came out of nowhere in Woodbury. That thing showed up as quickly as it left!" If he only knew! It brought a smile to many of us who had made this amazing sign happen.

Later that night, as a few of my friends were getting ready to leave, my mom told them to watch for signs from me. As they got into their car and turned it on, the song playing on the radio was "Stairway To Heaven" by Led

Zeppelin. My buddies immediately called my mom and told her what they were experiencing. Yes, I had made that happen by manipulating frequencies with my energy! I have this type of sign mastered, to the point where I teach it as a form of energy work in heaven. Because we are in a timeless dimension, we can plug songs in at just the right moment.

* * *

More and more family and friends were finding out about my death, which had me going nonstop. Intense emotions were everywhere I went. I had to help these people that I loved so much! I worked hard with dreams, giving them to folks who were able to sleep and who were not blocked by profound grief and emotional upheaval to the same extent as my immediate family. Our neighbor friend, Chris, came over and told my mom she had just had a dream of someone she knew casually who had passed on. In the dream, this woman had told her to tell my mom that her son was doing fine and not to worry. What a thrill it was when people would share these experiences, as it helped my family so much! I used my energy to get several brilliant red cardinals to gather outside my parents' window at the feeder. My dad had asked me to give him a sign that I was near. Then after the first red cardinal arrived, Dad asked if that bird was truly from me, then would I please send more cardinals. I did exactly that!

When my family and friends were told about "pennies from heaven" as a sign, I quickly began manipulating pennies and moving them with my energy to be seen at many places, wherever they went. Most of these pennies were just objects that I moved with the energy of my mind. Moving objects with our minds is easy for us, just as the wind or waves of an ocean move things with the force of their energy. In the same way, our mind-energy has a resistance, a force, that moves objects wherever we want them to go. The difference between our mind-energy and the wind is that we can be very precise with our guidance. This is neither difficult nor exhausting. I recall watching the movie *Ghost* when I was a kid. I now know that many of the things that occurred in that movie are possible for someone who has returned to heaven!

These signs and dreams helped to give hope to my family, which then made it easier for me to reach them from my dimension. It softened their grief slightly, which helped to raise their vibration to be closer to mine. Profound grief has a very low vibration, which makes it difficult for us to connect with loved ones on earth. When we leave the earthly dimension and transition back home to heaven, we are vibrating at a much higher frequency than before. We have to lower our vibration to get closer to yours in order to communicate with you, and the closer we can make our vibrations to yours, the more able we are to reconnect with you.

* * *

My funeral was a week after the accident. I was there, together with other loved ones of the family who had transitioned before me. It's true: we do come to our own funerals. Seeing my body in a casket was surreal! My family had me dressed in my favorite clothes, and I was wearing my trusty Minnesota Twins baseball cap. My favorite snowboard was propped up next to the casket, which I liked.

During the visitation service, many loved ones told stories about me. It was fun for me to listen in! My mom told the story about the arrivals of my MN Twins baseball caps, and how the song "My Sweet Lady" by John Denver had played on the CD player at exactly the time of her seeing each of them. She said she knew this was Mikey talking to her through the lyrics of the music. Mom told everyone that this song was the reason why she was still standing. As she played the song for all to hear, I don't think I saw a dry eye in the church.

I had a great time messing with my friend Lisa, who was telling the story of how Frontier Airlines had lost my luggage twice when I flew with them. Her cell phone started to ring in church as she was talking, and she tried to turn it off. For some reason, thanks to me, it wouldn't stop ringing no matter what she did! She gave the phone to her mom, who also could not get it to stop ringing. Her mom finally took it out of the church. You could hear it ringing even as she was taking it outside! It was hilarious, and Lisa said that she knew it was me messing with her. Oh, how I loved to tease her!

My funeral mass was nicely done. I appreciated that. Denise, our friend and neighbor from down the street, opened the service by singing what she called "Mikey's Song," a beautiful song she had written with my telepathic input that talked about God, and how we—who are all actually part of the Unity of God—are present with you. Father Dave allowed all the pallbearers to wear a Minnesota Twins baseball cap like the one I had always worn in life, with "Mikey" embroidered on the side. That was way cool! The homily was wonderful, especially when Father Dave told everyone, "Do you think he is sleeping up there? He's not sleeping! If Mikey loved snowboarding here, of course he is snowboarding there!" (Do you know what? He is absolutely right!) I was amazed to see all the people on earth who came to give loving support to my family and friends, and to each other. It pleased me so much!

After the funeral and burial were over, my family and a few other relatives went back to the church to gather up the leftover food from the luncheon. As they walked in, two custodians were standing over a vacuum cleaner that had just burned out. I had done it again! Despite being in profound grief, everyone started to laugh, and Frankie, one of the custodians, asked my family what they found so funny. They told him what had happened to the other vacuum cleaners a few days earlier, and they told him they knew I was the one who had done it.

Frankie smiled and said, "Well, this vacuum was working just fine until you all showed up! And since you all are into 'signs' like this, I need to tell you what happened to me when I was working last night in the chapel. I was closing up shop after the visitation, and I was assisting the funeral directors with moving Mikey's casket from the church back into the chapel for the evening. After I did this, I turned off the light in that room and closed and locked the door. As I continued to finish cleaning, I noticed through the glass door of the chapel that the light was back on. I thought that was strange, and proceeded to turn it back off and lock the door again. Later, I walked by the chapel and noticed the light on again. I actually wondered if Mikey wanted it that way. For the second time, I opened the door, turned off the light, and relocked it. After I finished my work for the night, I locked up the church building doors and went to my car. Before I left, I drove up to the doors to recheck to be sure they were locked. That was when I noticed the chapel lights were back on again! And you know, I was the only one in the building that night."

My mom and dad said, "He always had to have a night light on, you know." And they were right! I had so much fun watching Frankie that night as I played with the lights. But what was so cool is that he knew in his heart that it was really me messing with him!

CHAPTER THREE
BEGINNING MY NEXT STAGE OF LIFE

My job of reconnecting with my family was just beginning. I was meeting frequently in the afterlife dimensions with my guides, and with the guides of those on earth as they helped me figure out how to orchestrate this. I had a lot of work to do! Going back and forth between the dimensions did not take much effort on my part, but I will say that it was a crazy adjustment for me at first. I was trying so hard to comfort my family and friends on earth. Feeling their sadness was very troubling for me.

My immediate family and some of my friends quickly became huge believers in the signs that I was giving to them. I was so happy when they would share their experiences with others. And once they started to sleep better, I was able to connect and communicate with them directly in their dreams.

Something that you on earth may not realize is that you have the ability to travel outside of your body at night. Your soul, your spiritual essence, can actually meet with us in another dimension. Astral travel dreams are dreams you experience that are so real to you that you feel you are actually with us. Well, you are! We are meeting in the astral dimension, which is of a higher vibration than the earth dimension, but not yet to the frequency of heaven or the afterlife. These are communications dreams, and you remember them very well.

I recall telling my mom during a dream that I was not gone. I said that I was very close to her, and I could hear her when she talked to me. In that dream, I hugged her, and she really felt it! My mom knew she was truly with me during that dream experience. For my dad, I did a dream in which I appeared to be younger. I had Rocco, our family dog, with me. We both appeared young and vibrant. I wanted my family to know that our pets were safe and with me! My dad understood.

When Joey, my brother, was sleeping well, I came to the front door in his dream. I knocked, and he answered, saying, "Where have you been?" I told him I was sorry, and I grabbed him and gave him the biggest hug! I love my brother so much, and I wanted him to know that I am always watching over him. To help to confirm that, I influenced a girl at Joey's school to paint him a picture of me. We are able to put thoughts into people's heads telepathically. This was an acquaintance, but not someone Joey spent time with. My dad was always telling me out loud to "please watch over your brother. Please!" So one day, Joey came home from school with the portrait that the girl had painted of me. On the bottom of the picture she had put: "MJM (my initials) Always Watching Over." This really knocked my family for a loop! I was working hard to comfort them, and they knew in their hearts that all of this was from me.

I continued to give signs and dreams to my family and friends, and I was delighted that my mom was journaling everything that was being experienced. In fact, she continues to journal today! She gathered notebooks of information, as well as objects that I had altered to express my love through the symbol of a heart. When my mom went to the store JoAnn's to pick up decorations for my gravesite, I made the song "My Sweet Lady" by John Denver play over the PA system for her. I did the same thing for her when she went into a Walgreens. I followed her around with that song! Watching her reactions always brought a tear of happiness to my eye as she thanked me out loud for letting her know I was with her. And yes, these bodies that we have in heaven can cry. We have the ability to show all our emotions here if we choose to do that, perhaps more so than ever!

* * *

My family worked hard to gain control of their grief. Immediately after my passing, they set up a scholarship fund in my name at my Catholic high school, Cretin-Derham Hall, to help children who were in need of tuition. To fund this, they decided to organize an event that would raise money, and within nine months they held a Mikey Morgan Night during a Minnesota Twins baseball game. It was a very well-attended event, and seeing my picture up on the Jumbotron with Joe Mauer was a thrill! In the eighth grade, I had been his bat boy for two games when Joe had played baseball for Cretin-Derham Hall, so he and I had had a picture taken together, and that could be used for this event. Creating a silver lining and helping others during their time of grief gave my family strength and hope to carry on. They did this event five years in a row.

Another way my mom moved through her grief was by taking over my truck. She often talks to me out loud as she drives, and I can tell she has found comfort in doing this. The closer the loving connection, the more we can feel your emotions almost as if they were our own. She got personalized license plates for the vehicle that say "MYMIKEY." She tapes pictures of me up on the dashboard and has dragonflies swinging from the mirror.

After my passing, Mom received a small package from The Dragonfly Project as a gift from a friend. This non-profit corporation in Minnesota will send out a condolence card, a copy of the dragonfly story, and a dragonfly keychain as a message of hope to a grieving person or family when they are contacted to do so. Like butterflies, dragonflies go through a wingless stage before their nymphs transform into beautiful winged creatures. This life cycle can be seen to represent our loved ones who have transitioned to heaven, and that is what the "Dragonfly Story" is about.

Please know that while you are still on earth, you cannot see those who have gone to heaven ahead of you, but we truly do still exist, and we are closely connected with you. We have transformed, but we remain the same individual. Since my death, mom has been wearing dragonflies to represent our continued bond and connection. This really makes me feel good! And quite frankly, using dragonflies or butterflies as a sign is easy for those of us in spirit. I love to use dragonflies when the season is right, to give my family a shout that I am near!

We can herd up a big group, or we can have a single insect do something unusual by using our energy as guidance.

Moving insects this way is one more thing that really is easy for us. We literally push them around, like wind or a breeze would. Our energy has a resistance, a force, that moves them where we want them to go. The difference with us versus a wind is that we can be very precise with our guidance and control, where a breeze is more general and random. We can have one of these insects land on you, and have it stay for a while by using the force of our energy. Understand that the heavenly dimensions are all around you, just at a higher vibration. When we draw close to the earth by changing how we resonate, we absolutely have the ability to control even many insects together.

Even when it is not the season for dragonflies, we still can use them as a sign that we are near you. When my family was driving down the freeway and asking me for a sign, they all laughed as a truck pulling a U-haul trailer soon passed them. The trailer had a large blue dragonfly on the side. Again, timing of knowing this vehicle is coming up behind them and then putting a thought into their heads about me is what makes this type of sign a success!

* * *

As I continued with my efforts to advance the plan I had made with my mom to teach through the veil, I would move back and forth through the dimensions, enjoying time in heaven and then drawing back to earth to help my loved ones. I really was enjoying heaven!

I had loved to snowboard while on earth, and the mountains in heaven are amazing and beautiful. They are much bigger than the ones I saw on earth, with steep sharp peaks, stone details, and beautiful shapes. The snow on these mountains is abundant and brilliantly white, smoother than powder, fluffy and light. It is cold, because that is how snow feels in our mind. So as I was exploring soon after I returned from earth, I scanned the hills and mountains and noticed that there were people snowboarding and skiing out there. I asked one of my guides, "Is that snowboarding I'm seeing? Really? You can snowboard here?!"

I was told that yes, I was indeed seeing people snowboarding. These were individuals who had returned home and who continue to enjoy the sport. What we like to do on earth we can do here, too. The big plus is that if you happen to fall, there is no way for you to get hurt. It didn't take me long to simulate with my mind my favorite snowboard that I had on earth. I even put on my favorite tinted Oakley goggles to have the full affect! With just a thought, I was on that mountain, hitting the slopes. It was crazy what I was able to do on my board! I hit the half pipe (there was an actual half pipe, and it was far bigger than any I ever saw on earth) and was doing all kinds of flips, board grabs, and just sailing through the air like never before on a snowboard! I was even doing better than Shaun White. How sweet is that? They also have terrain parks here with rails, tables, and benches to do tricks on. What a set up! I soon connected with others who enjoyed this sport as we shared time in the mountains of heaven. We get together often now to snowboard. I can hardly wait for my buddies on earth to see what this is like!

I took up snowboarding when I was a freshman in high school, when I did not make the school's basketball team. I liked the sport because it was individual and very challenging. My dad was a good skier. He thought that maybe I would like to try that instead. But I preferred the snowboard, as I felt it took more skill to learn and it looked really cool! That was what all the young kids were doing, and I wanted to be a part of it. I practiced hard and became a good boarder very quickly. Soon I was instructing snowboarding classes at Afton Alps in Minnesota, and then I was a coach for one of their competitive snowboard teams. When we took a family trip to Colorado to check out the mountains for some snowboarding and skiing, I was totally hooked. I wanted to move there! That was when I decided that I needed to go to Colorado for college.

* * *

In heaven, I was sitting down often with my Higher Guides and taking classes from the Elders with other students who were at about my developmental level. I was continuing my work on spiritual matters that involve the use of energy, learning more about how various kinds of vibration affect others, and also how they affect objects in different dimensions. I was studying the infinite power of thought, and what it can create or destroy; variables in positive and negative energies, and their effects; and love, the many aspects of it and the dimensional effects that surround it.

While I am learning, I also am teaching and helping others here who have come back recently as they try to connect with and comfort their loved ones on earth. I enjoy drawing close to the earth level with them to help them learn to manipulate objects and electricity with their minds as signs to those they love. I don't ignore my own loved ones, either. I often draw close to the earthly dimension to keep in touch with them. I hear them asking for me. I love how they know our connection is still there! Remember, we never run out of time here. I can move in an instant to be where I want and need to be.

I appreciated very much the fact that my family would still talk to me out loud. That let me know their intent and what they needed. Often I still can hear them telepathically, especially when they are deep in thought about something that is concerning them. I can feel their emotions as well. The more loving the connection, the more prominent this ability is.

* * *

As some months passed after the accident, my ninety-year-old grandfather was declining more and becoming more forgetful, and my mom was becoming more involved in his care. She often asked me out loud for any help I could give. I visited him often. The cultural influences that he had experienced over his lifetime were diminishing, and he was becoming more open again to spirit. This type of thing often happens as we age on earth. The veil between the dimensions was getting thin for him. He was beginning to talk about how I would come to visit him at night. I loved my grandpa, who was better known as "E.I." by all of us grandkids because he used to play the concertina and entertain us with the "EIO Polka" song. I loved him, and I wanted to give him comfort in his final years on earth.

One day when my mom was visiting my grandparents and assisting my grandma with his care, E.I. asked my mom if she had a hat he could wear. He said he felt that if his head were warm, perhaps he would be able to think better. A few days later, my mom brought him one of my snowboarding hats and placed it on his head as he sat in his motorized recliner. E.I. loved it! As he rested, my mom went and got the groceries for my grandparents. When she returned, and after she had put the groceries away, my grandma wanted Mom to trim her hair before she left for home. They went into the bathroom to get that done. At this point, I infused E.I. with my energy! As my grandma sat on the stool in the bathroom, getting her hair trimmed by my mom, E.I. got out of his recliner and walked down the hall past the door of the bathroom with his rolling walker. He had a huge smile on his face. And he was wearing my snowboarding hat.

E.I. proceeded into his bedroom and asked my mom to take out his concertina, which was the musical instrument he often had played for the family many years before. This instrument was quite heavy. As my grandpa sat down in a chair, he asked my mom to place it on his lap. E.I. had not played his concertina in quite a while, but what followed was awesome! He immediately began to play the U of MN fight song. Then he played six more songs, some of them polkas, and his music was flawless. My mom and grandma could not believe what was happening. My mom called her sister and held the phone in the air for her to listen. They were all amazed!

When E.I. was done, he looked at my mom and said, "Look what Mikey is doing for me. He is working through his hat!" When he finished playing, my mom lifted the concertina off his lap and put it away. E.I. walked back down the hall to the living room with his rolling walker, still wearing my snowboarding hat. He walked over to the picture of me on the coffee table and said, "Mikey, thank you so much for what you did for me today!" He sat back in his recliner and immediately fell asleep. I cannot tell you how great all of this made me feel! And that incident with E.I. and the snowboarding hat was later going to be a key element in helping me bring my connection with my mom even closer.

* * *

Compassionate Friends is a support group for parents who have lost a child. My mom and dad went to a few of their meetings over the course of perhaps a year and a half after my passing, and there they met Mitch Carmody, who is a well-known presenter and grief facilitator for Compassionate Friends. Mitch is also on staff as a workshop presenter with T.A.P.S. (The Tragedy Assistance Program for Survivors), and he is the innovator of Proactive Grieving Seminars and the host of his own radio show, "Grief Chat."

One evening when my mom was at a Compassionate Friends meeting, Mitch was speaking about signs as a means of communication from your loved ones who have passed from this earth. The session was called "Whispers of Love." He asked if any volunteers in the audience would be interested in sharing a sign they had received from their child. I was thrilled when my mom stood up to share some of the signs I had given them. Mitch loved the sign I had done involving my grandpa with the snowboarding hat, and he asked if he could publish that story in his next column in the *Living With Loss* magazine. Mom agreed. She didn't realize it at the time, but this story was the first crucial link I needed to begin the process of reconnecting with my mom and establishing real communication between the dimensions.

Chapter Four
Reconnecting

Just knowing that I had survived my death was a comfort to my family, and it helped to soften their grief. But it was only the beginning! My main purpose in being born as Mikey Morgan and living that brief lifetime on earth had been so I could communicate with all of you through my mom. As her grief settled down and she became more relaxed and open, I was eager to begin. She swears now that she never signed up for this, but our work in teaching through the veil is something that she and I planned together with our guides before either of us was born.

My spirit guides helped me immensely with my efforts to reconnect directly with my mom. Signs and dreams helped to increase the overall openness to communication within my family, and I also worked telepathically with friends and relatives on earth to encourage my parents to see a medium. They needed to understand that this type of communication was possible. Putting thoughts into people's minds as if they are their own thoughts is easy for those of us who are more advanced, and within months I was putting thoughts into many people's minds to encourage my parents to see a medium.

My mom was scared when the possibility of seeing a medium first was suggested to her. She carried that old Catholic guilt from her strict upbringing. My dad was less hesitant, but for this plan of teaching through the veil to work, I would need to establish communication with my mom. Of course, she had no conscious memory of how diligently we had worked on our plan while we were still in heaven together. We hadn't realized as we did this planning how hard it was going to be for me to remind her of it! Over time, and with encouragement from various friends, my parents went to see a few different mediums. They had some good results and validation. They knew the information they received was from me, but still it was not enough for my mom to understand that she had the ability to do this type of communication herself. There were times when she thought she was able to hear my voice, but she assumed it must be wishful thinking. She didn't trust her psychic abilities at all. Soon I knew that I had to figure out something else.

Souls in the afterlife are very in-tune with mediums. We know who on earth has the ability to connect with us effectively. I communicated with several guides and loved ones and traveled through the vast dimensions of the afterlife to figure out the various mediums available and what they personally did to connect.

This was when I was guided to Sally Baldwin of the Dying To Live Again Foundation. She was a spiritual medium from Florida who used a pendulum with a small letter and number disc to facilitate communication with us in the afterlife. You could see what we were trying to say by how we energetically moved the pendulum over the disc toward specific letters and numbers. What was perfect was that Sally was planning a mother-child reunion retreat in Sun Valley, Idaho, for October of 2009. Discussion about signs and dreams would be part of it, but Sally's main focus was going to be to see whether bereaved mothers could be comforted by communicating directly with their children in heaven through the use of a pendulum. She was recruiting through grief groups, including Compassionate Friends, and she planned to pick seven to ten mothers in the United States for this event, for whom all expenses would be paid by a donor of the foundation.

I acted quickly. First I had to work with my spiritual guides and the guides of others to coordinate and influence a connection to occur between my mom and Sally. The window of opportunity for the retreat was short. We were literally working from all angles! The *Living With Loss* magazines with my grandfather's snowboarding-hat story had just arrived at Mitch Carmody's house, and he called my mom to tell her she could pick up some extra copies there. Ten minutes before my mom got to Mitch's house, Sally sent him an email about the retreat she was recruiting for. When my mom arrived, Mitch looked at her and said, "Carol, I'm tingling all over! I just got an email from Sally Baldwin, the spiritual medium from the Dying to Live Again Foundation, and she is recruiting moms for this all-expenses-paid retreat she is having in October. It's about signs and dreams, as well as communication with your child who has passed on. Here is the email. With all that you have going on with Mikey, you need to apply right away!" So my mom went home with her magazines, and she contacted Sally. I was thrilled!

I was persistent in working with Sally to convince her she had to pick my mom for her retreat. I communicated with her directly, and more than once! I truly believed if my mom could see what I was saying by how my energy moved the pendulum over the letter disc, she would know for certain that I was talking to her. I knew this way of communicating was going to work for us. No one in my immediate family harbored any anger or blame related to my passing, which was so important in establishing communication. Negative emotions lower a person's vibration. It is extremely difficult for us to reach and connect with our loved ones from our aspect in heaven when they are deep in anger or grief.

* * *

Many mothers applied for the Mother-Child Reunion retreat from all over the United States. My mom was indeed chosen, but after Sally contacted her to tell her she had been chosen to attend the retreat, Mom suddenly became fearful and hesitant. More Catholic guilt! She decided to visit her elderly cousin, a Catholic nun, for another opinion about whether communicating with the dead might be wrong. This wonderfully wise woman told my mom that she needed to go to the retreat. She knew that what my family had been experiencing with signs and dreams was real, and she felt that my mom had been picked for a reason.

My mom and dad both went to Sun Valley that October, which was a life-changing experience for each of them. My mom attended the retreat, while my dad did his own sightseeing.

As the Mother-Child Reunion retreat began, all seven mothers who had been chosen pitched right in and worked hard with their pendulums under Sally Baldwin's guidance. She gave them each a letter-number disc to use for word spelling with the pendulum. They did a ritual before they began, asking for God's loving guidance and protection. My mom's ability with the pendulum was apparent. Our loving connection was very strong, with communication beginning to flow. The combined energy was intense! I would draw very close to the earth dimension by changing my vibration to make this work. My mom was amazed at how well the pendulum moved over the letters as she held it still, and she knew in her heart that I was communicating with her. Sally had the moms start out with asking their children simple "yes–no" questions. I would move the pendulum in a clockwise motion for the answer "yes," and a counterclockwise motion for the answer "no." Mom asked me questions that related to me, and I gave her consistently correct answers by how I moved the pendulum with my energy. Sally then had the mothers ask their children to spell simple words by moving the pendulum to different letters on the disc and confirming them as accurate by indicating yes or no.

My mother and I have a very strong loving connection. It helps, too, that she never has blamed anyone for my passing, including God. Apparently that is rare. She didn't have negative emotions lowering her vibration and making it more difficult for me to connect with her. She always was able to feel that I was nearby and know that we were close. She was confident that the signs and dreams that I gave her were real communications from me, no matter what others said. It is the combined loving energy of my mother and me that makes our pendulum communication possible, with my energy guiding the precise movement of the pendulum. The channel between us is wide open!

The first full word I spelled for her on the letter disc was LOVE. And love truly is what it is all about here in heaven! My mom was able to feel my presence as we worked together by the strong tingling sensation that my energy would give her over her upper back, shoulders, and the sides of her face. It was especially intense on the right, as she used her right hand with the pendulum.

Early that evening, after the events of the retreat were done for the day, my mom called my dad on his cell phone (he was out sightseeing) to tell him that she could actually communicate with me in heaven. My dad didn't know what to think. My mom became emotional and began to cry, saying, "But I really can!"

She tried to explain how the pendulum worked, but he challenged her, thinking that it must be her own mind doing it. He asked my mom to ask me a question where her answer was always no, but my answer while I was on earth was always yes. So while my dad was still on the phone, my mom asked me if I still thought they should get a hot tub. This had been my family's big debate while I was on earth: my brother and I had wanted one, while both of our parents had not. I took hold of that pendulum and swung it so hard with my energy clockwise for the answer "yes" that it almost flew out of my mom's hand! She started to cry hard then, and she told my dad what was happening. You cannot imagine the emotions that I felt that day! I was overwhelmed with joy and excitement. It had taken me two years, but I was now able to communicate with my mom directly. Now our real work could begin!

When Mom returned home after the retreat, she was hesitant and wondering who would possibly believe that she could communicate with me in heaven. Mom was also concerned about how she would explain this to my brother, Joey. I was thrilled when she went back to visit her cousin, the gentle Catholic nun, to see what she thought. Mom sat down with her and showed her how she communicated with me by pendulum with use of the letter and number disc. I told them by use of the pendulum and disc that God is Love and that love is the basis of all that exists. Heaven is right here, and your loved ones are still close to you! Mom's cousin remained incredibly supportive, telling my mom what a gift she had and that she must never stop working with me. The message of love is so important, and people need to know how close our loved ones and heaven really are to those on earth! She told my mom that of course communication happens now. She said, "How do you think they received some of the information in the Bible? It had to come through somebody!" Hearing this gave my mom the confidence she needed to move forward.

* * *

Joey had entered college at Kansas University, but he was going to be home for Thanksgiving break in less than a month. I felt the need to help my mom with Joey in validating our communication ability. As I drew myself close to him in Kansas, I noticed that he was having dinner with our Aunt Deb from Texas, who was then passing through town. I listened to their conversation. Then I told my mom about their visit, spelling out the details on the letter disc with use of the pendulum. I suggested that my mom text Joey on his phone with what I had given her, and she did just that. Joey was shocked! He quickly contacted her and said, "There is no possible way you would know about this and our conversation. Aunt Deb just left right now!" Mom told Joey what I had told her about their visit. I had been right there with them. Mom then said, "I know this may sound crazy, but I can communicate with Mikey now. When you come home for break, I need to show you how."

Joey really did not know what to think at this point. When he came home from college a few weeks later, I talked to Joey with the assistance of my mom, by means of the pendulum. We kidded and reminisced about old times. What a reunion. I was thrilled!

I was so proud of my mom as she practiced every day with her pendulum for a good two years to improve our ability to communicate. Even if she only had a couple of minutes to spare, she still made the effort. To practice with the precision of pendulum movement, Mom would take coupons or a newspaper and have me spell things to her by how I moved the pendulum over the paper. She had me make small circles and then big circles. I would change the movement of the pendulum quickly in response to her requests. When Mom told me to stop the pendulum, I would; then I would start the movement back up again at her command. My accuracy amazed her. I could tell Mom was having fun with this, as she often smiled and said to me, "How can someone deny what is going on here? This is nuts! I can hardly believe what has happened to me." She knew she wasn't a magician. Mom knew in her heart it was truly me! Gradually, she was able to hear me telepathically as the pendulum in her hand spelled words. Over time, we became skilled communicators, and the pendulum moved with great precision! I would tell her full sentences telepathically, with Mom then confirming with the pendulum what she heard from me.

Using the pendulum made it easy for me to validate the signs and dreams that I was giving to her, so she knew that all of it was coming from me. Even though we had the ability to communicate using the pendulum now, Mom requested that I keep giving her signs. She loves signs! I have honored that request, and I continue to give signs to many loved ones on earth to this day. What I really appreciate is when my signs are acknowledged. It's an awesome way to get a message across, even if that message is nothing more than that I'm here and I love them still!

* * *

Knowing that my mom was pretty clueless about afterlife concepts, I started out easily giving her what I wanted her to know. Her only knowledge of heaven was what she had learned in practicing the Catholic faith. We were all raised Catholic, with no other religious influences. I found that the simpler I made my explanations of what I was now experiencing, the easier it was for her to make sense of them. As my mom told others about my messages, she gradually became more confident. I told her about our plan made before she was born to bring you the truth about your own eternal life, so I had needed to leave the earth in order to fulfill our plan. Mom would always insist to me that she never would have agreed to such a thing, but her attitude was softening. When I mentioned to her that I resided in the Sixth Plane of the afterlife, she had no idea what that meant. She thought everything that was happening to her was simply unbelievable, yet she always knew that it really was her own son talking to her.

Eventually, Mom started to invite family and friends over to show them how she could communicate with me by pendulum. They would sit around the kitchen table, and we would chat. Many were amazed at her abilities. Talking to my loved ones again through my mom's connection with me was so much fun! Sometimes I would even flick the lights on and off with my energy to get their attention. This is easy to do: my energy simply interferes with the electrical current that is operating the light. It's my interference with that current that causes the light to flicker or to turn on or off. What was the best was when my mom would have the radio on as she worked with me. Messing with songs to have certain ones play at precise moments during a conversation is my specialty. I just love electronics! When we draw close to the earth dimension from the afterlife, our energy can influence many things, especially anything electrical.

When my mom would have these gatherings, I would share during her pendulum demonstration basic information about heaven, and the fact that it is all about love. I kept the information simple. I didn't want to overwhelm my mother.

* * *

Mom continued to keep in contact with Mitch Carmody, and he told her about an upcoming conference in Phoenix, Arizona, where he was going to be a presenter. It was the First Annual Afterlife Awareness Conference, and he encouraged Mom to attend. This was key for me, as I needed my mom to meet someone who could help her with our plan. I encouraged my mom to attend this conference. She was new at this, and especially new at understanding the information that I wanted to give her. I knew through conversation with my guides in heaven that there would be knowledgeable people at this event. Mom decided to go, and to spend time there with two of the other mothers from Sally Baldwin's retreat. Mom flew down to Arizona and stayed at the Embassy Suites Hotel in Phoenix, where the conference was being held. She got there the day before the event began, planning on meeting the mothers from the retreat that night for dinner. My mom had some free time before dinner, and she knew the hotel had a happy hour. She thought she would go upstairs for a glass of wine before the other mothers arrived. As we were leaving her room, Mom briefly sat down and asked me aloud as she used the pendulum, "Mikey, please help me meet someone at this conference who can help me with what I am supposed to do."

I said in her mind as the pendulum moved across the letter disc, "I will do the best I can!" Mom went to the upstairs room where the happy hour was being held, and she found that the room was filling up. She got a glass of wine, and then I guided her to sit down at a small table that was next to another table with a couple seated at it. My guides knew that these individuals were related to the woman who was running this Afterlife Conference. I thought this might be a start for my mom to get my messages about the afterlife to others if a connection could be made.

Soon another woman came and joined the couple. There were guides with her who indicated that she was an enthusiastic individual who was well researched in afterlife evidence from various resources, including through respected mediums. She was assertive, yet positive in her approach. She had the ability to write, and recently had completed a book about dying and the afterlife. With this information, I felt that maybe she could be a key helper for Mom if somehow we could get them to connect. Understand that we who are in spirit often work together to get a common goal achieved. Literally things can just fall into place perfectly when several of us are at work to coordinate it. This is an example of true synchronicity at work from behind the scenes!

It really was perfect timing. Watching her, I felt this was the person I needed my mom to meet. She was bubbly and friendly in her manner, which I knew would make my mom feel comfortable. Her name was Roberta Grimes. As I watched, my mom listened to their conversation about the conference that was about to begin. I encouraged my mom telepathically to talk to this table. After a few minutes, my mom got up the courage to ask these folks a question.

"Are you all here for the conference? I came from Minnesota for it!"

Roberta immediately asked my mom what had made her decide to come. My mom said, "Well, I think I have an interesting story, and I don't know what to do with it. My oldest son, Mikey, passed over three years ago in an accident. I was one of seven moms picked in the United States to go to an all-expenses-paid retreat with spiritual medium Sally Baldwin in 2009. When I was there, she told me I had the ability to communicate with my son in the afterlife by means of a pendulum. And, you know what? I can!"

Roberta said, "Really? I would love to see it!"

So they agreed to meet in my mom's room the following day.

Roberta was quite surprised at my mom's ability with the pendulum. In fact, Roberta really did not think it was possible until she saw it for herself. But what was more fascinating to her was the information I gave during that session. Roberta knew my mom was clueless on afterlife concepts. There was no way she would have known what she was saying without my assistance.

During the conference, Roberta spent time with my mom. Afterwards, she encouraged her to participate on afterlifeforums.com, which was an internet discussion group forum about afterlife concepts. After she returned home, my mom did participate on the forum just a bit, but then she lost her confidence. There were some very knowledgeable folks on the website, and Mom had no idea how to confirm what I was trying to tell her. Roberta soon contacted Mom and told her she needed to get back on the forum. She said, "Mikey needs a place to share what he knows. Don't be nervous. So far, he hasn't made a mistake. I've spent forty years studying the afterlife, and I'm starting to think he knows more than I do!"

So Mom returned to the forums, posting regularly the information that I was giving her. Soon there was a section established where people from all over the world could ask us questions. This was exactly what I wanted! It is a great way to teach. My mom's confidence has really improved. And as she has become more confident, I have been able to give her information in more detail.

* * *

Over the past five years, I have been giving my mother a lot of information about the afterlife, or heaven. She has accepted this knowledge with an open mind, although she hasn't done any research on the subject. And as she cautiously shared this information with others who were well researched on the topic, she began to realize that there was something to what I was saying. It was the fact that the experts kept telling her what I was saying was true that gave her peace of mind.

Before I was born as Mikey Morgan, I had had no further need to incarnate. I had not been in a body for many years. The last time I was here was in the 1600s, and that life was an easy and fun adventure: I was a musician who played string instruments. My love for music obviously carried through to this most recent lifetime! But although I had made good progress on my own spiritual journey, I could see now that many people on the earth plane needed to learn what really is going on. I could have tried to communicate from there through mediums, but I thought that wouldn't work very well. I had to get used to life on earth again so I could talk as one of you, and I wanted to be able to talk through someone with whom my love connection was strong. Of course, my mother doesn't remember this, but before either of us was born, we agreed that I would come in as her first son and live a brief earth lifetime so she would be still pretty young when I died and I would be able to communicate through her.

And it's working well so far! We are establishing my mother's credibility just as many good people all over the earth are working together to bring the truth to light. It won't be long now! Mom is gradually becoming more confident. She knows that I'm real, but she has a lot of doubts about herself.

Not long after we started using the pendulum, Mom was being filmed by a local producer in Minnesota for a documentary he wanted to make about us. But when we came to the last filming session, the person who was working on it had a family medical need that interrupted production. We never went back to finish it. The timing simply wasn't right. We had been using the pendulum for just seven months, and Mom still had trouble believing in what we were doing. I was worried that someone would criticize her and make her completely lose her confidence. I didn't want her to become so fearful that she would stop our work! Over time, as she becomes more ready for it, we'll become more public with our message. Everything with our work together is progressing according to the plan. To date, Mom has been on numerous radio shows, several of them with Roberta Grimes, sharing our story, including the signs and the information that I have shared with her about heaven or the afterlife.

Please know that it is all about love. When it comes to heaven, love is all there is! The afterlife or heaven is totally structured on love. As I move about through the vast number of dimensions that exist by changing the vibration of my being, I see how the scenery and structures transform. Amazing! I am just taking it all in. It's like first seeing the Rocky Mountains on earth: having had that brief earth lifetime as a kid, I feel as if I'm seeing everything freshly. It is so obvious as I travel about that the more loving we are, the higher the vibration is of the dimensions where we can be. And the higher the vibration is, the more dramatically beautiful it is! I'm going to try to explain all of this to you from my perspective here in heaven, but I don't know how I ever can really make you understand how it feels to be where I am now, safe and free amid so much beauty, and living in joy and overwhelming love.

Chapter Five
How the Life-Planning Process Works

Spiritual development is highly individual, but most people evolve spiritually by living repeated lifetimes on earth until we reach a level of development that will allow us to continue to develop spiritually by helping others to progress. I had lived many lives on earth. I was long past the need to ever incarnate again, but conditions on earth were troubling me more and more. Many of us at the higher levels are troubled! There is a consensus in heaven that there is work to be done to shift spiritual truths in a positive way in the earth dimension. Basically, we've got to raise the vibration of the dimension where you are, and now. Violence and killing, judging and ridiculing over beliefs or other trivial things is wrong. That isn't what God or love is about! We have come to realize that many of us will need to step in and help from various angles. And I had been so long away from the earth when I decided that I wanted to try to help you that I thought I should spend another brief lifetime on earth so I could talk to you as one of you. I enjoyed my lifetime as Mikey Morgan, but it had been only a means to my end of being able to teach on the earth plane.

* * *

So, how does this all work, anyway? How come we go back and forth to earth or other places, and then return to heaven? Why leave heaven in the first place, and what is the process by which we do this? Let me tell you, if we are eternal beings (which we are), then a baby on earth actually is not a "new soul," but is a soul from heaven who probably has lived many times before and is coming again for the experience of another carefully planned earth-life.

There are an infinite number of souls and soul groups that travel together in the vast dimensions of all the many universes that exist. Together they enjoy all kinds of experiences that help them to progress spiritually. We all are actually fellow space travelers, just like on *Star Trek!* We come to earth to learn about life "in the physical," with the many experiences that it has to offer. It is on earth that we have the opportunity to experience and exercise our free will in both positive and negative ways.

Not everyone from your soul group comes at the same time. Understand that these soul groups can be very large!

Some members will stay back, and some will help with guidance. Spiritual growth seems to work best when we work mostly within our soul groups, so that is most common. People in our own soul group will have a similar vibration or energy to ours, although each soul group will have people at various levels of spiritual development.

Before we come to earth, we sit down with many souls from our group and work on what we would like to experience. It all boils down to a general life plan with a few key events that we want to take on. There are actually conference halls where we do some of this work! Much effort goes into this planning, as we will be taking on complex new roles in this next life journey. Sometimes we will mix with other soul groups to achieve the experiences that we feel that we need. I can remember doing this with my family (we do pick our parents and family) before we started coming to earth to get this plan going. We were all so excited to take on our new adventure! It seemed so temporary, like just a short run when we planned it in heaven, but when we got to earth, it took on a whole new feel. Our free will and the free will of others can alter things along the way, but each of us has spirit guides in the afterlife levels who help us to stay on track.

Each person on earth has at least one primary spirit guide, although some people have many guides. Generally, guides are a bit more spiritually advanced than the people they are guiding on earth. Our guides are most often from our soul group connection, and they can change during our lifetimes. For example, now I am one of my mother's key guides. I have joined the primary guide who began with her at her birth. She and I, as well as my dad and Joey, have shared many lifetimes together, taking on different roles and experiences. We are of the same soul group, and mom and I have a strong soul or spiritual connection with each other that is matched for pure service to God.

* * *

I can remember hanging out with Joey in heaven as I waited for my opportunity to be my parents' first child. As soon as the timing was right, I committed myself at conception with the silver cord (our energy/spiritual connection from our soul), merging with the embryo of my new earthly shell. This cord or projection of our energy is what attaches our soul to our body. When the attachment occurs, life in the physical body begins. During my mom's pregnancy, I (my soul, or "being") went back and forth as I continued to work with my guides and loved ones in heaven on my plan for what I wanted to accomplish during my new brief lifetime. It is the silver cord that allows this type of communication to happen with our soul, which is our being, or "who we are." Our soul can leave our body as long as this cord is intact. This type of easy communication stops when the birth process starts.

Being born is quite the experience! I could think of better ways to arrive on the planet. Not the most comfortable thing I have encountered. In fact, there is pain involved. It can be quite frightening, coming out into the world! It is definitely a shock to our spiritual nature. Adjusting to our earthly body is not so easy, either, but being held and cared for lovingly helps a lot. Our ease of movement is now cumbersome. No wonder I cried so much!

When we are very young, the veil between heaven and earth is thin for us. We are still intensely connected with souls in the afterlife, and often we are able to see them and hear them. Have you ever noticed a young baby staring intently, as though it is seeing something, yet you can't see what has the child's attention? Or the child might be smiling at something, yet there appears to be nothing there? You may even think, "Oh, the baby must have gas." It is very possible that baby is seeing and hearing from other souls in the afterlife. This can continue on into early childhood. Our "imaginary friends" can actually be real! As we age and are exposed to life on earth and the rules of society, this openness often diminishes. For some, however, the door does not fully shut. It is these individuals who are more connected, intuitive, and psychic in nature. There is nothing wrong with this, as we all have the innate potential for this type of connection. After all, we are all threads interwoven in the tapestry of life through all the dimensions.

As we become elderly and approach our deaths, the veil again thins for us. Openness returns, and the channel expands. This can be a time of visions, dreams, and loving communication that gives comfort to the individual who is about to transition. Our loved ones come to us and guide us back home. We are never alone during the dying process, no matter what age we are when we leave. Much love surrounds us. Our loved ones who have gone before us are very aware of our arrival. Death of the body occurs when the silver cord severs with the soul detaching.

Why do we bother to go through all of this? To learn about love in many different ways! We can grow spiritually in the afterlife levels as well, but it is just that earth's challenges are tougher and therefore give us greater potential for growth. We can gain much more on earth because there is the influence of both positive and negative ways. We therefore have more choices with the challenges. We truly are exercising our free will constantly.

Spiritual growth is equivalent to how we vibrate or resonate with our energy. The more positive or loving our actions or ways with any given experience in our life, the higher the vibration. Again, everything is energy, including us. There are infinite life challenges and experiences on earth. Rarely are two completely alike. It is how we react, how we treat others, our true intent of what we are doing and how we act in that situation that makes the difference.

Positive ways = higher spiritual growth = higher personal vibration.

On earth, there are many different types of love that we can experience with our different relationships and interactions. Romantic love, parent-child love, neighborly love, family love, love of yourself, general love for a stranger, love for your country, love for a pet, love for an activity, love for a sport, and so on. The type or degree of love can be very different, but it all has to do with love, and all forms of love are positive in vibration when it comes to spiritual growth. Love really covers many things when it comes to our actions: caring for each other and for ourselves, respecting and forgiving one another, not judging others, helping and being considerate and kind to others with our actions. Being civil, not rude. Taking good care of ourselves. Basically, treating someone or something as you would want to be treated. The Golden Rule. Simple, really!

Another way to put this most important lesson of all is to say that love equals spiritual growth. There are so many aspects that involve love as the basis with our interactions and general way of how we act in our lives. Anything positive has love as the basis. Just a smile alone is positive! Simple kindness and respect in your approach are examples of this. Positive ways brings positive ways, while negativity brews negativity. Having negative ways brings down our spiritual vibration, and then love is no longer the basis. You can actually feel it when someone around you is being negative or hurtful. Life on earth is a gift that has potential for great spiritual growth! It is very important that we always respect life.

To tell you the truth, it is all about sincere and ever more perfect love! Love that has a general understanding and caring for another. Love that is respectful and kind. Love that is sincere from the soul and has the ability to forgive and never judge others. Love is the Force of all creation of what exists, and it is infinitely powerful. The more loving we are, the more glorious it is for us in the heavenly dimensions.

Mikey with his dad, brother Joey, and
good friend Dan at Copper Mountain in 2004

Mikey wearing his first
baseball cap at age 3

Grandpa E.I. playing the concertina for his grandchildren
when he was in his early 80s

Mikey with his family at the overlook at
Lake Dillon near Copper Mountain

Mikey and his mom at the Mother-Son Dance
at Cretin-Derham Hall High School in May 2005.
Mikey called this event the "Mom Prom."

Mikey and Joey loved to go boating and jet skiing together

Mikey and Joey at the top of the American Flyer LIft at Copper Mountain in 2005

"Mikey Mo" working as the DJ at
Washington's Sports Bar and Grill in 2007

Mikey with his dog Chelsea.
They loved to play together!

Mikey with his signature baseball cap in July of 2006, fourteen months before his death

Mikey loved to play baseball. This sport was a huge part of his life, especially during his grade school years. This picture was taken in 2001.

This rainbow was a sign given to Joey when he visited Copper Mountain in March of 2015. His mom had told Joey to watch for signs from Mikey, as Copper Mountain had been his favorite place. After Joey went up the Super Bee Lift at Copper Mountain, he got off the lift and turned around to see this amazing rainbow! It lasted for 2 hours. Mikey later told their mom by pendulum that he had created this spectacular sign with the help of several afterlife friends.

Chapter Six
God is Love

God = LOVE = The Source of all that exists. That is all that we need to remember. God is way beyond anything the human mind can possibly comprehend. God is far greater than a man with a beard sitting in a big white chair and judging everyone who returns to heaven! But you know, that is how I remember God being portrayed when I was on earth. It makes me laugh when I think of this now. Maybe it is because God is called "He" in the Bible, which makes it seem that God is a man. The Big Guy. Who knows? Certainly I can tell you that God does not strike us down or punish us. God truly is a Unity of Absolute Pure Love, which is Infinite. And there is no limit with God. This Unity is The Source or Collective of all that exists. Mind, Consciousness, whatever word you choose to use. We are all part of this Unity. The more loving we are, the more God-like we are.

People in heaven are aware of God. Soon after they return to heaven, they realize that God is far greater than just one man. God is part of everyone and everything. God is everywhere, and you can feel it! God is at every level of reality, but most intense at the Celestial levels. Truly, the more love (higher vibration) or positive energy, the more God there is at that level or aspect. The more negative and lacking in love (lower vibration), the less God there is. The outer darkness level is the lowest vibratory level of the afterlife, negative and low in love, so very little of God is there.

I am what is called an Advanced Being, someone who has progressed well into the higher realms of existence and often teaches and helps others as they work toward achieving their own spiritual growth. But there are a few beings who are Ascended Masters, who have completed all experiences necessary to be One with the Source. Jesus and Buddha are two of the greater Ascended Masters that came to earth. I know that Christians think Jesus is going to come back, and that is very likely to happen once we have followed His teachings enough to raise the vibratory rate of human consciousness. This is all part of the "spiritual shift" that is occurring. Believing in Jesus alone is not your salvation. Living what He taught you is! He told us how to live, and now that is what we are supposed to be doing. If you hope for a Second Coming of Jesus, then live as much as possible exactly as He taught you to live!

It's important to remember that religions are man-made institutions, with man-made rules and practices. God doesn't have rules or dictate what we should do. God wants us to learn to love more perfectly, because that raises our vibration and draws us closer to our Source, which is what God is. There is nothing wrong with religion as long as love is the basis, without judgment of the beliefs of others. The only religion in the afterlife is LOVE. In the afterlife, individuals relate to God by showing loving ways in everything they do. Individuals still pray here, since prayer is a powerful thought which is part of the work of the mind. People here pray both individually and in groups.

Demonstrating loving and positive ways is what increases our loving vibration, and that is what progresses us spiritually. In fact, this is the driving force of why we choose to come to earth, or to one of the other places and dimensions that exist. The one way we truly learn things is to experience them! Talking about it is not enough. You could say that earth is actually our school. We come to earth to learn, and we may choose to return many times, again taking on an earthly human shell. It is on earth that we take on a gender. If we are the same gender for several lifetimes, and then later come back to earth as the opposite gender, sometimes the influences from our previous life gender bleed through. Realizing this may help to answer gender identity questions, as well as give a better understanding of homosexuality on earth. Déjà vu feelings also are bleed-through experiences from a previous adventure on earth.

* * *

Learning to love more as God loves is the reason why we live lifetimes on earth. Everyone in heaven craves spiritual growth, and spiritual growth is all about learning ever more perfect love. It's something like learning to drive a car: people can tell you how to do it, but you can't really learn now to do it unless you get behind the wheel! So at first, making much spiritual progress generally happens when we live earth lives. Gradually, as we progress through the fourth and fifth aspects or levels, we become more able to continue our spiritual growth while we remain in the afterlife levels, just by studying and helping others. Reincarnation always is optional for us, but until we get to Level Five, nearly all of us have a strong desire to reincarnate. By the time we reach the upper fifth aspect of spiritual development, most of us remain in the afterlife levels. Unless, like me, we take it into our minds that doing another incarnation will make us more useful to advancing the spiritual development of other people!

You should know, too, that there are many other dimensions and some planets where we can choose to incarnate in order to learn better spiritual growth. But the earth plane is especially tough, with the influences there of ego and materialism, so spiritual growth can be rapid on earth. Ego can be one of the biggest obstacles to spiritual growth in the earthly dimension. When our ego gains too much control over us, spiritual growth is difficult. Often with a strong ego comes the mentality that we feel that we are better than others, and we are superior. It can make us quite judgmental and critical of others. The feeling of superiority makes us feel powerful, and this can influence our behavior into more negativity. Controlling others that we feel are below us, or not as worthy as we are, makes us feel good. We begin to feed off the power and control of others, and we enjoy it.

The individual with a strong ego always thinks he is right, whether he is or not. There is an arrogance that develops. With this comes hurtful and sometimes cruel behavior and actions toward others. Materialism can fuel this even more. There can be materialistic rewards to this negative behavior that further influence the individual to act this way. They see the material reward as positive for themselves, not looking at what they did to get it, or who they hurt along the way. Wars can result in extreme cases, as these individuals try to totally dominate others. When this happens, the individuals being attacked try to defend themselves and protect others from these negative ways. It is very important for each of us to keep our ego in check, using it in positive ways for the benefit of others and ourselves. Materialism can be used in positive ways as well, both for ourselves and for others. Often it takes money on earth to be able to help another person, and to achieve benefits at a higher magnitude.

People on earth are often fearful, but really, you have nothing to fear! What negativity exists is almost all on earth, and all made by people. Here in heaven, and in most of what exists, there is nothing for you to fear. Always remember that the higher your vibration, the more aspects of heaven you can experience and enjoy. Higher-vibration souls can go lower, but those of lower vibration cannot go higher. They miss out on so much. Hence the strong desire for spiritual growth!

CHAPTER SEVEN

THE LEVELS OF THE AFTERLIFE

Heaven is an awesome place with an incredible number of dimensions to experience. It is plain cool! There are seven categories or planes, with thousands of aspects or graduations within each, all based on differences in personal vibration, which is entirely based on love. Again, the higher your vibration, the more advanced you are spiritually, and the more glorious the dimensions you reside in. Love is the basis of everything that is positive in nature. Basically, positive = higher vibration. Negative = lower vibration. When we are respectful, kind, non-judgmental, forgiving, civil in general, helping others, and are not rude or hurtful, we are being positive and loving.

Whatever dimension of the afterlife you are experiencing at any given time, that environment will be solid and real to you. In fact, it is more real than being on earth! It is more real because it is a place that is true to our inner being of who we truly are. When we are on earth, we are in a dimension that is lower in vibration to how we normally resonate. We take on a physical form that is not true to our spiritual nature of how we normally vibrate when we are at home in the afterlife. We are weighted down when we're on earth. When we shed our earthly shell, we soon realize that the heavy laws that govern the earth—gravity, time, decay, and the heaviness of its matter—do not apply to us anymore. We are free, and it is what feels right and true to us!

Texture is the same in heaven as it is on earth, so your pets will feel the same to you; water or snow or fabrics will feel the same. What really feels different in heaven is love. It is everywhere, with a warmth and comfort that just overwhelms you! This is often described and felt in near-death experiences. What those individuals having NDE's describe is an accurate feeling of love as it is experienced in the afterlife.

In all the afterlife dimensions, there is no concept of time. We live always in the "now." Time restrictions and limitations do not exist. Our vision is 360 degrees, and we hear and communicate with others telepathically. But that doesn't mean that it is silent in heaven. Sound is incredibly clear and distinct here!

We can choose to appear to others however we like. We often take on the appearance of our last lifetime, looking like we did in our prime years. However, we can appear to be older or younger if we choose. There is no actual gender in heaven. We are true spiritual beings. We have no internal organs. Internal organs pertain only to the physical body while we are on earth. We can appear to be solid in heaven, or we can choose to be more transparent at times in our spiritual body. It's up to us! Our bodies are solid energy, and are created by our minds. We hear, see, feel with our minds, which are our consciousness or true being, and we communicate telepathically with our minds.

In heaven we can reach out with our hand and touch something and feel it, but understand that hand is part of our energy that is part of our mind, which is our true being. A hug in heaven is a hundred times better than a hug on earth! The exchange of sincere love in heaven is far superior to any love act on earth, and that includes sex. Spiritual beings literally merge together with their energies in an explosive reunion of incredible vibrations of love! It is the most intense pleasure you can imagine because it is love made manifest.

It is important to understand and remember that everything is energy. You, me, everything, and everybody! What is being experienced on earth, and what is being experienced in heaven: it is all energy. Your soul is a highly vibrant energy, but even your desk at work is energy at a low and dense rate of vibration. How we appear and look in heaven is how we resonate with the energy of our soul. Whatever the case, we will always know each other by the unique loving energy of our being. We look and feel solid. Personally, I choose to appear in earth-clothes most of the time, with my trusty Minnesota Twins baseball cap on. And my hair is still as auburn as it can be!

The afterlife or heaven has an infinite number of realms or dimensions which are based in the seven planes, categories, or divisions. Try not to think of these planes as on top of one other or linear because that is not how it is. They are all over the place! Each one is based on its own vibration, with the slower vibrations closer to the earth's vibration and the faster, more intense vibrations being higher and more advanced.

The two lowest planes or levels of the afterlife are often referred to as the "outer darkness." Some may refer to this as hell. One important thing I want to point out is there is no eternal damnation. Hell in the sense of eternal damnation does not exist. There is not one individual Satan, just as God is not one individual man. There are, however, negative and non-loving energies or entities. Nasty dimensions of low vibration that are filled with negativity do exist, but there is always loving guidance to assist these souls if they choose to improve themselves and increase their loving vibrations. We can always exercise our free will. These two lower planes or aspects are dark, dreary, and with limited light and love. The souls there are in agony within themselves. Loving souls attempt to help them and guide them, and some will accept the offered assist, while some are determined to stay in darkness.

The outer darkness is not a pleasant place to be, and I personally do not visit those dimensions often. I will go there only to assist someone who specifically requests my help. There are spiritual beings dedicated to this area that work very hard with the individuals who reside there, trying to get them to understand the importance of positive ways. Much effort is needed, but it still is a choice if the individual wants to improve. If they do, then there is much work to do, as improvement comes through experiences and choosing to act in a positive way. We need to demonstrate and live it through our actions, and work for spiritual growth.

Those on the very lowest levels have trouble even perceiving people who are at higher vibratory levels, which makes getting help to them even more difficult. Sometimes we might ask the newly dead to help out by visiting the lowest levels, since people who have just died can be perceived more easily by those in the outer darkness than we can. But that effect is short-lived, because the newly dead are still raising their spiritual vibratory rates, and they very soon rise to a vibratory level that the lowest-level beings cannot easily perceive.

Planes three through five are often called the "Summerlands" of the afterlife. These middle planes are where I often hang out. They are where most of the fun-filled post-death activity is. Love, light, incredible colors, nature, and scenery! The flowers will even turn to greet you. Everything is so alive with love. There are beautiful buildings with many activities going on. We live in houses here! At higher levels there are few houses because there is not much need for shelter, but when you have recently died it's nice to have that familiar feeling of walking in somewhere and closing the door.

There are many dimensions to the Summerlands, and individuals can enjoy all kinds of nature, architecture, music, and activities that they enjoyed on earth. In fact, there are even areas where people recapture the feeling and details of what it was like when they lived on earth. Like attracts like. Beings will group together and celebrate those particular times that they remember. Individuals will even appear with clothes on from the era of earth-time they are celebrating. The buildings and architecture will be similar to that era in time, as well as the vehicles used, so if it was a time when horses were the main way of transportation, there will be horses and carriages. There are pastures, fields, and forests. There are mountains, trees, greenery, and flowers in brilliant colors. There are rivers and lakes. There is no sun, but light that feels just like the sun gives us warmth and comfort. The sky color can vary, and it even can be more than one color. Sometimes the sky will appear to be made of rainbows!

* * *

Whatever your favorite hobbies might be, you will find people here with similar interests to connect with and enjoy your fun times together. This is where I do my snowboarding. Some of my friends are from my soul group, and some are not. So we can include everyone; even those of us who have progressed to higher spiritual levels will come to the midlevel Summerland levels where friends of lower vibration are comfortable.

There are group activities and games that souls participate in as well. I will never turn down a chance to play baseball or beach volleyball with others. Generally, it's for pure enjoyment versus competition. We prefer not to get mad at the umpires or referees! All the sports that you enjoy on earth can be played in heaven. Individuals with similar interests get together for the enjoyment of the game. You can play games to win, but there never is the feeling of superiority associated with winning that there is on earth.

It's fun to see how much music is loved in these dimensions. Many musicians and artists who have passed from earth continue to entertain others here. There are concerts galore, and the music is incredible. It's "heavenly" in all respects of the word! In fact, many song lyrics heard on earth are actually channeled in from individuals in the afterlife planes of existence. Often songs you listen to on earth are giving you messages about heaven and what is truly important, and those messages come right from the souls here in heaven.

We enjoy music here from many eras of earth-time. In addition, there is music of heavenly quality that has not been heard on earth—beautiful melodies of richness and harmony. There are musical instruments of all kinds—strings and brass—that appear similar to instruments on earth, but nothing is played out of tune! There is flawless singing as well. Music and concerts are generally played in open areas, with the music giving off colors and images that can reflect messages of love. Being famous on earth doesn't make a performer famous here, but some of those who enjoyed playing and entertaining on earth often do it in heaven. Personally, I have seen Elvis Presley in action and have connected with John Denver.

Most advancements in technology have their beginnings here. Scientists in these dimensions work things out and actually channel in information to scientists on earth. Progression in phone technology has gone crazy, especially since I left earth! Individuals working on technology in the afterlife connect with individuals in the same fields on earth and work closely with those people's spirit guides. There are techno-geeks here just like there are on earth. And here it all is done by thought, through trial and error. Because the dimensions vary in vibration and in how things work, new innovations are designed here through trial and error, but the last stages of development have to occur on earth once the information is received there telepathically.

Transportation or travel in heaven can be by thought (which occurs in an instant), on foot, or in a vehicle. Crazy, but true! Most of the vehicles here will be found in the Summerland levels. You should see what some folks drive or fly in. Cars can look like a favorite car they had on earth, or like a car they wanted to have, but could not afford.

Planes can look similar as well. Some folks have fun in what looks like little space ships or saucers. You can ride a bike. You can have a boat in the water. You can ride in a hot air balloon. In every case, it is the person's own energy that propels the vehicle, so there is no exhaust. Since people here can travel by thought, they don't need to drive or fly a vehicle, but they want to! Just like individuals who enjoy cars and planes on earth, that interest can continue when they return back home.

* * *

I want to tell you about the beautiful children that come back home to heaven. I know the loss of a baby or young child on earth is truly one of the most difficult things to bear. The heartache and pain is intense. But please know that when these children transition to heaven, they are treated like royalty! The incredible love and light of God surrounds them and embraces them. They are cradled and cared for by many loving souls, including souls who are connected to them by loving relationships. The children are comforted in a very special place within the beautiful heavenly dimensions that is specific to their young needs. These realms have buildings of grandeur with beautiful and gentle scenery all around, and play areas that are beyond your earthly comprehension. It is a place of adoration. I visit these dimensions often, as wonderful work goes on here with so many. Gentle and kind learning continues for them. This is where you will often find Jesus spending time. Jesus loves the children! Angels also spend time here. Their loving, gentle ways bring such consolation and joy!

When children first transition, there is often confusion, wondering what is happening to them. Immediate guidance and loving service is there to give them comfort of great magnitude. We do not want children to be afraid in any way. They are quickly guided to this loving place. This heavenly dimension designed for children also has dwellings that look like storybook cottages that are very welcoming and familiar to children. There are young-appearing animals here like what they knew on earth, very loving and friendly. It is a happy and joyous place. Teaching the children has a focus on kindness, with the influence of positive ways in the interactions that occur with everyone there. It is simple, yet powerful in the approach on love.

Miscarried and aborted babies are a bit different than children who were on earth for a period of time and then transitioned back. Aborted babies lost the opportunity to complete the plan that was initially intended for them. Miscarried babies may be part of another individual's plan.

In both situations, these babies are in more of a communication mode with the spiritual realm, and are still quite connected, as they have not been born. So they do not go through the same degree of confusion or need to understand what has happened to them as children who had been born and started to live life on earth when they came back home.

Miscarried and aborted fetuses adjust more quickly, and soon return to the heavenly dimension that aligns with their vibration. They also can progress spiritually. They know their parents and families, and as the family members they left on earth also return home, some wonderful reunions occur. With aborted fetuses, those reunions can be tough for the parent who chose to end that child's life plan before its birth. A lot of planning had gone into that life that was ended by the parent's choice, and the guilt that the mother feels can be hard to get past. Of course, the child has long since forgiven the parent and shows her only love and kindness.

You cannot begin to imagine how wonderful the reunions and celebrations are when the children who have grown spiritually here see their parents and family members again as they too return home. Tears of joy flow everywhere! I have witnessed this many times, and to feel these emotions brings happiness that cannot be compared.

* * *

All animals live in harmony in the afterlife, and all our pets are with us! They wait for us patiently, happy and healthy and with their same personality. Often a beloved pet will come with other loved ones to guide us back home. While they wait for us to arrive, they live in a beautiful place or dimension where loving souls live with them in a village and watch over them.

I can remember reading the story about the "Rainbow Bridge" when I was on earth. Someone gave it to us when our dog Rocco died. The story talks about a beautiful place where our pets reside in heaven until we come and get them. Well, it is the absolute truth! You will be reunited with your pets again. I cannot tell you how special this aspect is. Truly, this village where the pets wait for us is one of my favorite places to visit in heaven! Soon after I returned home, I went to get my dogs, Chelsea (the golden retriever) and Rocco (the standard poodle), who had transitioned before me. I was drawn to them by the loving energy connection that we have. You cannot imagine how thrilled they were to see me! Chelsea immediately wanted to play fetch with her green tennis ball. Some things never change!

* * *

The Sixth Plane carries out much of the teaching that happens in the lower dimensions of the afterlife. There are many aspects to this vibratory plane, as there are to all the other planes. Again, the more spiritually advanced and loving, the higher the vibration of that aspect or dimension within that plane.

Plane Six has many aspects which focus on teaching. Much guidance comes from here and is taken back to the other planes or dimensions of heaven or the afterlife. It is a progression upward in vibration from the other planes, and it holds awesome buildings, universities, individual dwellings, and landscaping. The scenery is indescribable. Everything is majestic with brilliant colors that dance with life!

The Sixth Plane is intensive, as it has a primary purpose rooted in devotion to the growth of others through the teaching that it gives. It is high in energy, and those who live here have many different kinds of abilities. We are working together to achieve a common goal, and the focus is always on love.

Love is such a strong force here on the sixth level. You can literally feel the energy of it through your entire being! And with this force comes increased ability within those who reside here, and a shared deep knowledge and understanding. This is my home base. I spend time here with my higher guides, being educated on afterlife concepts. My Elders are my main advisors. I have shared experiences with them in many dimensions, and some of them even incarnated with me many years ago. While on earth, they have been my friends and relatives. They are wise, knowledgeable, and very caring in their work. Their knowledge comes from the many experiences they have had, as well as guidance from yet higher beings that are more evolved and advanced.

There is so much to learn! I am being educated on how various vibrations affect beings and objects in different dimensions, as well as the power of thought and what it can create or destroy, which is infinite. I study variables in positive and negative energies and their effects, and the many aspects of love, together with the dimensional effects that surround it. I also do a fair amount of energy work, which is the practical application of how various vibrations affect other people and objects in different dimensions. That is how we deliver many of our signs. I take this knowledge back to the Summerlands, where I teach others how to manipulate frequencies on earth to give signs to their loved ones.

You would be surprised to see how busy I can be with delivering signs and helping others to deliver them. My family and some of my friends are certainly aware of my ability with signs from heaven. What I love is when they notice a sign I gave, and they acknowledge it to me! I will confirm it with a surge of my energy that will send them goosebumps for sure. I have great fun with this, especially with a special few relatives and friends who are totally tuned in! I also work on improving my connection with my mom, and how to proceed with the teaching I would like to accomplish. What she and I are doing is coordinated with many others for the timing to be right. The gradual spiritual shift that is occurring now on earth is a group effort by many guides!

From the Sixth Plane, we go to other dimensions, teaching love and forgiveness as best we can, and we often encourage others to accept further earth-lives in order for true knowledge and understanding to be obtained. Mobility on Level Six is most often by thought, versus with use of a vehicle. When I am on the sixth level, I usually wear spirit robes rather than street clothes and my baseball cap, and I look a lot more distinguished! Our appearance is how we choose to resonate with our energy. Even if we choose not to look physical, we always know each other by the vibration or energy that we have and express to one another.

* * *

The Seventh Plane is the Celestial aspect of heaven. Heaven on the seventh floor! It is the home of the most advanced souls, and to my understanding it is beyond what the human mind can comprehend. Its incredible beauty and radiance and energy are beyond my ability to describe. This is Absolute Pure Love with all that exists. Complete Oneness with God, the Source. Perfection in love! Angelic in nature. It's the completion and understanding of all experiences, with full knowledge. To those who live there, it may seem somewhat physical, but not in the solid way that things seem to us even up through the Sixth Level. To my knowledge, the Sixth Plane's upper aspects or dimensions also are intense with loving energy, being close to the Celestial Plane.

The Seventh Plane—the Celestial Plane—is brilliantly and beautifully intense with loving energy that is infinite and powerful! We become one with God = Source, but we are yet individual in our true being. I like to use the rose flower as an analogy. We are the individual petals wrapped and woven into true perfection of love of the Highest Degree = God = the complete and perfect rose flower. I feel that is the easiest way to understand it, although it is beyond what we can comprehend with how great it is. I wish I could tell you more, but I'm not there yet and I don't have the ability even to visit the seventh level.

Are we just beams of light on the seventh level? Are we just one big energy ball? No! We are far greater than that. We are individual, yet One. And this One = God is of amazing power over all that exists. If Celestial Beings choose to go to a lower vibrational dimension, they often will appear solid to us, but that is their choice. When we reach the Celestial Level, although we are One with the Source, we remain individual. And we have reached total knowledge and understanding of all that exists.

I have to emphasize again that love is the underlying basis of everything to making spiritual progress. Every action, thought, word, and deed that is positive in nature has to do with love. There are many types of love, as discussed earlier, but each and every aspect of each type of love and the action and vibration that goes with it is positive. Nothing about love ever is negative.

The Archangels reside on the Seventh Level, but they also travel about to other dimensions. Archangels can present with wings, and some wear magnificent gowns that flow with grace. They are the heavenly helpers who give totally of themselves to guide and assist others in loving ways on their journey. The seventh-level dimensions are of the highest frequency of the afterlife. This is where our spiritual growth is taking us. Souls in these dimensions are very advanced, with incredible ability and power. But still their growth continues. It is infinite in its potential!

As I say, I am not there yet, but one thing I know is that although from where I am now, it appears that on the seventh level we will have attained perfect knowledge of all that exists, we are given to understand that growth and learning will continue forever. Just like learning and growth on earth continues, so it happens in the afterlife levels. Did you on earth twenty years ago ever expect the computers of today? So even at the Celestial Level, progression will continue that is beyond what the human mind can imagine. I don't know specifically how much more I have to do to reach the seventh level. I just keep focused on the task at hand!

Chapter Eight
The Post-Death Process

When we return to heaven, each of us has a life review with our higher guides. This review is for teaching and learning, with the loving guidance of the souls who are assisting us during the process. Souls who have recently arrived will get to see and feel the emotions of other souls that came from the interactions they had with that individual. So if we have harmed someone or acted in unloving ways, we can find that our life review is quite unpleasant in spots. It is almost like watching a frank and thorough movie of one's self. Of course, no one is perfect, and life on earth is difficult. And as we go through our life review, we are never alone, but we are actually reviewing and judging our life just passed with the love and support of our higher guides. It can be emotional with both joyous and unpleasant events. Always know that it is the intent of the individual's actions that matters most!

Instigating a negative act is very different from defending yourself against a negative act. The underlying intent is very different between the two. Again, positive actions (which have love as the basis) have a higher vibration, which progresses us spiritually. Negative actions have a low vibration. If our ego shows up at this review, and we cannot see certain actions as negative to others, teaching and guidance from the souls assisting us comes into play. Work with our higher guides must be done. It is a time for complete truth and sincere honesty. We need to learn and understand the aspects of our actions and behaviors, as there is a vibrational component to all of them. In some cases, if there was a hard life issue that we need now to better understand that involved another individual while we were on earth, that individual also may be present at the review so we can work it through with guidance. Our life on earth is for us to learn through our experiences about making choices in loving ways.

Education is continuous, with a focus on spiritual growth and other advancements in the many dimensions of heaven. Scholars in all areas teach many things, just as is true on earth. We all have jobs or tasks that we carry out, and we also have recreational activities that we enjoy. Relaxation is a must here, too! And wonderfully, the stress for the need of money to survive does not exist.

Life in the heavenly or afterlife dimensions is busy for me. We have plenty to do! I am constantly moving about, changing my vibration, to get to where I need to be. When

I hear or feel that my loved ones need me on earth, I am there. When I am needed for further teaching and guidance from my Elders in the higher realms, I am there! It is all about how I change my vibration of my true being that makes this work. And when it is time to have some fun, I am hanging out with my buddies here in the middle dimensions of the afterlife, and doing some serious snowboarding in mountains that are over the top amazing!

One thing I again want to emphasize is that whatever heavenly dimension you are experiencing, that environment will be real and solid to you. The wonderfully complex and amazing place where I am now truly feels more real than what you see around you on earth.

* * *

Once I settled back into my heavenly routine, I could not help but notice that there really is no religion here. (No politics, either!) At least, there is no religion as we know it on earth. Organized religion, with all its rules, is really just a human thing. The use of fear tactics to gain control over the people in the name of God is not what God is at all!

Everyone returns to heaven, no matter how they worshiped God or what they believed on earth. It is how we act that is most important. Understand that there is nothing wrong with any religion on earth, as long as it has love as the basis, and with no judging of others' beliefs. Unfortunately, this has not been the case from the time that religions started on the planet! Power and control of the people has taken a strong hold, it seems. Certainly this is not what Jesus, Buddha, Ghandi, or other advanced and enlightened souls taught when they were on earth. The killing and wars that have gone on over the centuries over religion are not what God is about. The Golden Rule to treat others as you want to be treated is really the only rule! Actually, the one true religion in heaven is LOVE. Do me a favor and listen to the song "Love is my Religion" by Ziggy Marley. Those lyrics have been channeled in to people on earth from here!

* * *

There are other vibrational dimensions that exist outside of the earthly dimension, but are not fully in the afterlife dimensions. NDE's (near-death experiences) and OBE's (out-of-body experiences) are adventures in another dimension beyond the earth, but people having them are not actually in the heavenly dimensions because their silver cord is intact and their body is still alive. It is not a full transition into the afterlife, the way that death is. The silver cord (our energy/spiritual connection) is what attaches our soul to our body. It is a projection from our true being, and it is the connection that gives us the ability to leave our earthly body and travel with our soul to certain dimensions that are not fully in the afterlife. OBE's can occur in a dream, or in a meditative or hypnotic state. NDE's can be experienced when our human body is close to shutting down and may be near death. In both scenarios, we are able to return to our body without death occurring because the cord remains intact. Therefore, NDE's and OBE's may have strong influences of the true heavenly dimensions, or they may not. These experiences do vary with those having them. Whatever the case may be, these experiences are very real to that individual soul! In fact, we can come from the afterlife dimensions by altering our vibration and join you during the NDE or OBE. Vivid dreams are the same way. I have done this several times with family and friends. Astral travel at its finest! Much communication can occur in the astral realms. Very real experiences, where you truly see and feel what is happening. Really, the sky is the limit with all the dimensions and the universes that exist!

Extra-Terrestrials (ET's) are inter-dimensional travelers that can show up as quickly as they disappear. This is possible by how they alter their vibration. When they become compatible with the earth's resonation, you can see them. They are like us in that we are all part of The Source = God. They just may appear with a different shell on than we do, but they are beings on a spiritual journey as well. Overall intentions can be good, with curiosity being a driving force. Also possible is their seeking of ways to assist people on earth. Actually, we also can be considered ET's, as we too come from one dimension (the afterlife) to another (earth), and then return again when our time on earth is done. Understand that there can be negativity as well as positive energy in all entities. Positive, loving ways will always be the most powerful force!

Chapter Nine
Some Answers

Heaven is where we spend nearly all of our eternal lives. And yes, our lives really are eternal! The one thing you can know for sure is that you never will die. And the second thing of which there is no doubt is that the more loving you become, the happier you will be, both on the earth and here in your true home. You can fight it. You can think there are other ways to make yourself happy. But for everyone there is only a single source of every good feeling, and that is learning how to love more in the way that God loves.

As I wrap up my book, things are occurring to me that you probably are wondering about. I'm going to use this chapter to answer as many questions as I can think of to give you a better understanding of how we see and comprehend things from our perspective here in the afterlife.

DO I MISS LIVING A PHYSICAL LIFE?

One thing that I really miss is eating. Give me a Chipotle burrito! I loved food when I was on earth, but there is no need to eat in the afterlife. When we first arrive here, we often feel the need to eat, and we want to eat. We can eat whatever we like here, but it's not really the same because we never get that "full" feeling. The taste comes from our memory of how things tasted when we were on earth. There is less satisfaction because we never get hungry. Because of that, we gradually lose interest in eating.

The other thing that I really miss is the close relationships I had with my friends and relatives who are still on earth. Many of them are losing their memory of me now, since they are so immersed in their earth lives. Of course, we'll be together again, but I wish they knew how alive and how close to them I really am! I send signs to them, but often people don't notice them or realize that they are signs from me, so my efforts are wasted. Our loving connections never end. Communication is possible in many different ways. There is great doubt among many, and it is that doubt that I intend to work on now to replace with knowledge, and then with joy.

What About Sex?

I died on the earth when I was twenty years old. I know how powerful the sex drive is, but it is entirely of the body. Sometimes sex can be a negative and violent act on earth. It is not always associated with love as the basis. We have bodies here in the afterlife that feel natural and healthy and never need to rest, but they don't have a sex drive. That makes a huge difference! Understand that a hug in heaven is 100 times better than a hug on earth. The exchange of sincere love in heaven is far superior to any love act on earth, and that includes sex. Spiritual beings literally merge together with their energies in an explosive reunion of incredible vibrations of love! It is the most intense pleasure you can imagine, because it is love made manifest. And believe it or not, this is only one pleasure in a place where we have so many wonderful things to do, and an infinity of time in which to do them. You think while you're there that sex is important, but when you get here, you will realize that it really wasn't important at all.

How Bad Is It for Us If We Commit Suicide?

The intention of our actions is what is always noted with everything that we do. For example, suicide can be disastrous for spiritual growth, or it might not be if it is committed because, for example, someone is mentally ill. Mental illness is no different than physical illness: both can take lives. With physical illness, we seek treatment and help. We need to do the same with mental illness. With both scenarios, sometimes treatment and counseling does not help, so death can result.

Some people, too, will risk or even voluntarily give up their lives in an act of pure love to help someone else. Soldiers in defensive wars protecting loved ones and homeland fall into this category, as do people who step into a bullet's path or fight to take down the shooter in an effort to save the lives of others. People have been killed by speeding cars while in the act of pushing a child out of the way. All such losses of life that are motivated by love are not suicides, but rather they are loving sacrifices of self in service to others.

Some suicides, though, are not the result of mental illness or of loving sacrifice. They are committed out of spite or revenge or deliberately to hurt another person. Or perhaps someone is giving up on a hard lesson without even trying. These situations can be tougher, but always, your intent is what is important. Taking others with you during the process would of course make things even worse because you feel the pain and agony not only of those you have left behind, but also of the loved ones of all those you took with you. This can be overwhelming.

Much loving guidance and teaching is given to people who come here after killing themselves. They really need help, and there are advanced beings who take on this responsibility. Once they realize all the effects of what they did, the remorse can be intense! When we return to the afterlife following a suicide, we realize that after taking our physical life, we are just as alive as ever. Sometimes this is quite the surprise to the individual. People who have killed themselves always start out in a common dimension within the Summerlands, where the focus is on counseling. As they progress, they return to the dimension that resonates with their vibration. For some, it is a very involved process. Their remorse at what they've done and their desire for forgiveness can be overwhelming.

TALK ABOUT HOW YOU TEACH OTHERS.

When I teach in the Summerlands, it might be casual and one-on-one, or it might be with a group in a classroom setting. I often work with people who are newly arrived here, helping them learn to deliver signs and make connections with their loved ones still on earth. I call it energy work, since what it amounts to is helping them learn to use the increased energy that they have now to affect things in the earth dimension. I teach them how to mess with electricity, how to move objects and guide small animals or insects, or how to give a loved one a feeling of their presence with tingling goosebumps. It is all done with the focused use of our energy. I teach them how to use the fact that we are not under the restraints of time to set up and deliver signs that will make people on earth really take notice.

CAN YOU TEACH PEOPLE TO DELIVER APPORTS?

Those who are a little more advanced can learn to deliver apports to their loved ones. Remember that everything is energy! And apports are just energy-produced items brought to the earth dimension when we here in the afterlife change the item's vibration. It's a process similar to inter-dimensional travel. Altering the vibratory rate of an object can make it move into a different dimension. When something becomes compatible in its vibration to that of the earthly dimension, it can be seen and appear as solid. Again, altering the vibration of an object or an individual can cause it to move and appear in a different dimension.

WHAT DO YOU WEAR IN THE AFTERLIFE?

The way that folks dress or appear in the afterlife is pretty much location-dependent. You will see civilian-type clothes more in the middle dimensions, depending on what activities are going on, and more robe-type dress in the teaching areas and universities. I would never wear a robe snowboarding! I wear clothes like what I wore on earth for that. In areas where folks are enjoying a particular era of time from earth, they will appear in clothes from that time frame. Actually, I change it up, sometimes wearing a robe when I am working with the Elders, then wearing casual clothes with my baseball cap when I am in other places. We always appear in civilian clothes when greeting loved ones who are transitioning.

The basic heavenly garb is a floor-length, long-sleeved tunic that's belted—think of Jesus, or an angel. People sixth level and above mostly wear those tunics, which are sometimes called spirit robes. In areas of teaching or university settings, you will see different-colored robes to indicate our level of knowledge. I always wear spirit robes when I am on the sixth level, and I look a bit older and more distinguished. My spirit robe is goldish in color. Sometimes you do see hats as well, but I don't wear one with my robe.

Do some in the afterlife have regrets about their lives?

I do meet people here who have regrets about their lives. That often can be the driving force that makes them want to go back to earth and try again. Once we return to the afterlife, we recall the bigger picture of why we were on earth in the first place! The most common regrets seem to be that people when on earth cared too little for others, or were very judgmental of others. Personally, I don't have real regrets about my last lifetime. I accomplished what I hoped to accomplish, and now I can much better teach on the earth from here. In case you wonder, I have no intention of ever going back to the earth again!

Is there such a thing as sin?

Sin is just a word. It's a word used by humans for certain acts that they have labeled as bad. It holds onto the influences of judgment, so it is of the earth. In the afterlife, all actions are based on vibration only. The more loving the action, the higher the vibration; the less loving, the lower the vibration. There are no specific acts that are sins in themselves. The notion of rules that have to be obeyed or we are committing a sin comes entirely from human thinking. Our actions are either positive or negative. To be negative, to be lacking in love, produces a reduction in vibration in us and in those around us, and this ultimately can affect the earthly dimension in a very negative and harmful way. To be unloving is worse than you can possibly imagine! But it isn't a sin. It is a setback. It hurts you, and it hurts everyone else on earth for you to be negative, nasty, bitter, unloving, or anything other than positive and loving and forgiving. But still, it isn't sin.

IS THERE JUDGMENT?

The time that I spent around a table with my Elders (Higher Guides) right after I got back, examining the life I had just lived, is how judgment happens after you die on earth. Neither God nor any other figure judges you as bad, but you examine critically the life you've just lived and basically you judge yourself. Nothing goes unnoticed when it comes to relationships. I will say, however, that if you do not recognize certain acts as non-loving or hurtful to others, loving guidance and teaching comes into play. We do not get a "pass" simply because we cannot recognize our own unloving actions. It is always a time for learning with our Higher Guides. We basically have work to do to understand this more fully. And we learn best through experience. Every act has a vibrational component to it.

The more positive our actions, the higher the vibration that goes with us on our journey.

Forgiving yourself is so important! All of us make mistakes. You came into the life that you're living now with a plan to learn and grow spiritually, and maybe with a plan to accomplish certain things. If you begin right now to really apply yourself to your life plan as you understand it, then your judgment should be a happy time.

What Is the Outer Darkness?

The outer darkness is the low-love vibrational dimensions of the afterlife that individuals end up in if they have negative and non-loving ways. It is truly self-induced! We do reap what we sow. This could be thought of as "hell," but please understand that there is no eternal damnation and God does not put us there. When we have our life review with our Higher Guides, if our ego stays with us and we do not recognize our actions on earth as negative, guidance and teaching will come into play. It is all about learning. That is why we come to earth, and we do not get a pass just because we don't think that we did anything negative. We are taught and given loving guidance in an effort to help us escape the outer darkness levels, but in the end we do end up in the dimension that fits the vibration of our being.

If people want to place themselves in the outer darkness levels because they're having trouble forgiving themselves, yet their vibration is of a higher dimension, then work needs to be done with them to understand they need to forgive themselves and progress forward. There are specific individuals (guides) who do much work in this area. It is important that you know there is no eternal damnation! We can always improve ourselves if we choose to. There is loving guidance always available to us.

What are Angels and Archangels?

Archangels are Celestial beings that are of the very highest vibration, but will leave their natural dimension to help and guide others. Angels are also high-energy beings, although not as advanced as the Archangels. They also help and guide others, both on earth and in the other dimensions. They are of a different "class or soul group" (for lack of a better word) then we are, and they do not incarnate. They are part of the Source, just as we are. Why are there different classes of beings? I'm not sure. My impulse is to say that is just how it is! Our spirit guides often do similar work as the Angels when it comes to helping us on our journeys. Sometimes when these Angels or Guides really need to make an impact with their ability to help us, they can literally appear just as quickly as they can disappear in the earthly dimension when they match up their vibration to the earth's. This does not happen often, but when it does, they will commonly resonate their energy to "look" just like a human being on earth. What can follow in their brief visit can seem miraculous!

TELL US ABOUT JESUS AND OTHER GREAT RELIGIOUS FIGURES.

Jesus is truly one of the greatest teachers that has ever come to earth. Jesus came to teach about the importance of love, kindness, forgiveness, and not judging others. He was murdered for trying to teach the truth. Because of how advanced spiritually Jesus was, He had great ability to do the many miracles that are recorded. We are all children of God, or part of God. We are all part of this Unity. So yes, Jesus is a part of God, but it is where Jesus came from that makes the difference here. He is of a very high realm of heaven. Understand that we all return to heaven, no matter what we believe or what religion we follow. "All are welcome with Jesus!" It is living by what Jesus taught that gives salvation in regards to spiritual growth. Saying that

He is your "Savior" alone does not give spiritual growth. Carrying out what He taught certainly does!

When Jesus presents himself in other dimensions, He often appears with wavy dark brown, almost shoulder length hair, and with a beard that is not long. His skin is darker in color, more of an olive or medium brown, but not white. He often wears a cream or white tunic-looking robe or garment with a rope around His waist when He is teaching. Jesus now resides in the Celestial dimensions, as does Buddha. However, they do appear in and visit the other aspects or dimensions of heaven.

Buddha also is very spiritually advanced and was a great teacher, encouraging similar aspects about love, respect for others, and kindness, just in a little different way. Both Buddha and Jesus did say that we reap what we sow. Positive ways brings positive; negative ways brings negative. Both lived a more humble life on earth. Buddha did teach about reincarnation, and this was also indicated with Jesus, but those teachings are not included in the Bible that exists today. Both also implied that with humbleness and suffering comes the potential for spiritual growth. Buddha focused on this throughout much of his life. Jesus spoke of The Beatitudes as an example of this in His teachings. Both of these spiritually advanced men taught well. It is what they taught as to how people on earth should live their lives that is hugely significant for us all! What you believe is what you believe, but that doesn't do much to bring you spiritual growth. It is how you live that will ultimately make the difference for you spiritually.

DO OUR BODIES IN HEAVEN EVER GET SICK OR OLD?

There are no true bodily illnesses in the afterlife. An individual may appear with a limitation that they had on earth, but it is not a true limitation. It is only how they are resonating their energy. Same thing applies to aging. There is no true aging.

DOES THE VEGETATION IN HEAVEN REALLY LOOK EARTHLIKE?

It looks a lot like the earth, but so much better! The vegetation is incredible, with brilliant colors, and it never fades or dies. It was created by very advanced beings with their combined efforts. The more advanced a being is, the more it has this creative ability. There is no limit with God = the Source of all that exists. All of this creation, both on earth and in heaven, is a combined effort of the Source, or God. These High Advanced Beings that are One with the

Source have amazing power and ability. They create through their powerful energy.

HOW IMPORTANT IS FORGIVING OTHERS?

Love is what is most important, and forgiveness and love go hand in hand. Forgiveness is really for the one who is forgiving, not for the one forgiven. When we experience negative actions from another that we feel are hurtful, the longer we hold on to the anger and frustration their actions cause in us, the more it actually pulls down our own vibration. But when we truly forgive, we let go of all the negative feelings that are associated with the action. Forgiving does not mean that we approve of the negative action, or that we have to like it. It is just letting go of the negative emotion or feeling that is associated with it that is so important. We need to put those emotions on a boat and send it out to sail and let it go!

Negativity of any kind pulls you down. This is huge when related to death and grief. If you hold blame and anger related to the loss of a loved one, that pulls you down so low, to a point where we cannot reach you for signs and communication. Your personal vibration goes in the tank! Hanging on to these emotions does no one any good. It changes nothing. The situation is the situation. Hanging in negativity is not healthy, either. If there are individuals in your life that continue to be hurtful or negative in their actions, if you try to change things for the better and it just doesn't work, often it is better to move on. You have your journey and they have theirs, and that is OK. But negativity brews negativity. Positive ways bring positive ways. Forgiveness is for you. It is the ability to let go of any negative feeling toward another due to their actions, and to move forward in a positive light. This is what raises our vibration. Positive ways = loving ways!

WHERE IS GOD?

God is present wherever there is love.

The Celestial Plane, becoming One with the Source, is the highest level or plane. However, even the Celestial Plane continues to offer progress within itself. As I understand things, the Celestial Plane is infinite in its potential! Spiritual growth continues forever, and that includes in the highest plane.

Chapter Ten
Carol Morgan Talks About Mikey's Earth-Life

This book is Mikey's story just as he told it to me from his perspective in heaven. Although I swear I never would have signed up for this, he tells me that before I was born, we agreed that he would come to me as my oldest son so he could die early and then communicate with you through me for the rest of my life. I found this very hard to believe at first. I still find it hard to believe! But the gentle and loving boy that Mikey always was turns out to be more alive now than he ever was, and he has taught me how to help him communicate with you. It's not in my nature to put myself forward this way. It is definitely not in my comfort zone. But when a beloved son asks something important of his mother, she tries. And I am trying!

He has asked me to write a chapter about his life on earth from my perspective. Doing that has been helpful, actually, in my efforts to process all that has happened.

* * *

Mikey was born on April 10th of 1987 in St. Paul, Minnesota. He was a darling baby, with a very round head and a button nose. Mikey's eyes were dark brown, and the little hair he had was like peach fuzz. He had a precious smile that would melt your heart.

During the first year of his life, Mikey experienced numerous ear infections. This was very challenging, and affected Mikey's moods due to lack of sleep and pain. When he was eleven months old, he ended up in the hospital with rotavirus. Mikey was very sick, and we worried for his life. When he recovered, we were so thankful. But from this point forward, I always worried that something was going to happen to him.

From early on, Mikey had a sense of humor, and he loved to be silly. He would sit in his high chair and pile food on top of his head, waiting for everyone's reaction. He would giggle and wiggle! Mikey did have his moments of being fussy, crabby, and throwing a few tantrums. He was a typical young child. But once his ear infections were under control, his personality really blossomed! He became a good listener and tried hard to please his parents.

As a young toddler, Mikey had a fabulous imagination and excellent vocabulary that was noted in his play. Ninja Turtles were a big hit, as well as his "wrestling buddy," a big stuffed toy that looked like a wrestler. Mikey loved to pretend he was wrestling like the guys on TV. He watched the World Wrestling Federation. It was a popular show with the kids when he was a little boy. He became very interested in basketball, playing for hours each day with the little basketball hoop we bought him for his birthday. He progressed his interest in sports, starting to play baseball by age 4. It was rare to see him without a baseball cap from this point on. He loved to play with his cousins and neighborhood friends. Mikey also enjoyed spending time with our family dog, Chelsea, a golden retriever. She loved to play fetch constantly, and Mikey would throw the ball for her.

When Mikey was four, his younger brother, Joey, was born. When we came home from the hospital, Mikey wondered why Joey cried so much. At first, he wanted us to return him. But it wasn't long before Mikey began to love his brother dearly, having fun with him and trying to make him laugh. They developed a strong bond and got along very well. There was minimal fighting or arguing with these two brothers. They enjoyed being together, playing, and having fun. Going sledding in the snow, being at a park on the swings, or on a boat ride at the lake or on the St. Croix River were some of the favorite times they shared. Joey loved it when Mikey would sit down with him as they drove little matchbox cars all around the house. Their imaginations soared as the cars came alive with their playing. Mikey always told me he didn't want any other siblings. He wanted it to be just him and Joey. The two brothers!

Mikey was an average student in grade school and high school. He worked hard to get B's. He was thrilled to get an A. His love for sports continued, and he was on the basketball, baseball, and soccer teams at St. Pascal's Grade School in St. Paul. During the summers, he played traveling baseball as well. Mikey worked hard on his athletics, practicing often and becoming quite good. It really came naturally to him. Before his baseball games, Mikey often wanted me to play catch with him to warm him up. I tried my best, but Mikey always reminded me that I threw a baseball like a girl. And I would kindly remind him that I was a girl! We had fun attending his games. Mikey made many friends on the different teams. When he graduated from grade school, Mikey received the Sportsman of the Year Award for athletics. He was thrilled with this honor!

It was during grade school that Mikey began to be interested in the music that was on the radio. He started to ask for specific CDs with the various songs for gifts, and he wanted his own CD player. The one song that was truly his favorite in grade school was "I Saw the Sign" by Ace of Base. He played this over and over. Mikey was definitely starting to show an interest in the lyrics of songs, and what message was being relayed through the music.

Mikey went to Cretin-Derham Hall High School in St. Paul, MN, a Catholic school known for its academics and its sports. Mikey had hoped to play basketball and baseball during his high school years, and as late fall and early winter approached, he tried out for the basketball teams as a freshman. He practiced hard, working on his skills. To our surprise, Mikey did not make any of the freshman teams. He came home from school that day shocked and devastated. Never did he realize how hard the competition would be. We were all sad, but this lasted only about a week. Very soon, Mikey decided that he would take up snowboarding instead!

Mikey never hung his head for long. He would move on. His dad thought that maybe skiing might be better, but Mikey was on a mission: his new sport was going to be snowboarding. I drove him to Afton Alps in Minnesota, where he quickly learned how to snowboard. We bought him a snowboard for Christmas, and off he went! Within a year, Mikey was working as a snowboard instructor at Afton Alps, and loving every minute of helping others learn his new skill. He did so well that Afton had him coach the junior competitive snowboard team. Mikey was thrilled when they won third place in an event during his first season of coaching!

Before Mikey got his driver's license, I would drive him to his job in Afton. He insisted that we play the song "The Middle" by Jimmy Eat World in the car every time we drove out there. Mikey told me the song fired him up for snowboarding, and he loved the message. As I listen to the song and lyrics today, it feels profound to me to realize what actually was going on and what was going to unfold in the years to come. The lyrics would also be for his mother, to give me strength on my new journey and role after his passing.

When spring arrived, Mikey tried out for the baseball team at Cretin-Derham Hall and made it. He was thrilled about this accomplishment. Mikey made some of his closest friends with the members of this team. This group of guys stayed together through high school and the few years of Mikey's life that followed. Mikey had these friends at our house often, which was fun for us as well! Mikey attended school dances and other events. He loved to be involved.

My favorite high school event was the annual Mother-Son Dance. Mikey called it the Mom Prom, and he said that everyone should go. He was a good sport. He danced with his mother a lot. We had so much fun together! Mikey enjoyed singing the songs as we danced. He had a few girlfriends in high school, all short-lived. He did go to prom his junior and senior years, as most of them did. Mikey was kind and very respectful to women.

During Mikey's freshman year in high school, we took our first family trip to Colorado for a skiing and snowboarding vacation in the early spring. What a family trip! The boys were amazed at the mountains and the beauty that surrounded them. Mikey fell in love with the place, telling everyone it was the best snowboarding he had ever seen! He wanted to move there, and soon he got the idea that Colorado was where he was going for college when he graduated from high school. We continued to go to Colorado every winter / spring for our vacations, developing family traditions along the way. Putting in the John Denver CD and singing the songs as we drove up interstate 70 was a big one. It truly was a "Rocky Mountain High"!

We really had no issues with Mikey as he was growing up. He never got into any trouble in grade school or in high school. He was a kind boy, and he was rather sensitive. Mikey always wanted to talk when he needed help or guidance of any kind. Not much was held back with him. We had a wonderful parent-child relationship. He was known to help out his friends and give them rides to various places after he got his driver's license.

Mikey easily showed his emotions. He could get frustrated, but then he would pick up the pieces and move forward. He definitely had the ability to forgive, but Mikey did avoid people that he felt continued to be negative or hurtful to him. He sustained a few injuries during all of his sports adventures, but he would work hard to get better. Then he was always back at it again.

Mikey was raised as a Catholic and attended Catholic grade school and high school. As a family, we attended church on Sundays. Mikey was never thrilled to go to Mass, and he often would have preferred to stay home. He believed in God and Jesus, and that there was life after being here on earth. Mikey was not very interested in the rules of the Church, however, and he actually questioned some of them. He certainly did not like it when people were pushy with their religious beliefs. It made him resist religion all the more!

* * *

During Mikey's senior year in high school, he applied to the business school at Colorado State University in Fort Collins. He toured a couple of different schools in Minnesota and Colorado, but his heart was set on CSU. With effort, Mikey got accepted there. We all went out to help Mikey move in for his freshman year. He was thrilled! I remember him telling me as he grabbed me by my shoulders, "Mom, can you believe it? I am actually going to live in Colorado!" Mikey knew very few kids when he first got to Colorado, but it didn't take him long to make new friends. He joined a fraternity and became very involved in its activities. Mikey loved everything about the college experience!

I should mention that Mikey did have a steady girlfriend for a while in college. They broke up a couple of months before the accident, but they still were in contact. I hope it helps her and all his friends to know that he still loves them and looks forward to seeing them all again.

Mikey did a lot of snowboarding every chance he could get, but he also knew that he needed to get a job to help pay for his extra-curricular activities. He ended up getting hired at Washington's Sports Bar and Grill, which was in the old town area of Fort Collins near the CSU campus. It was a place that was patronized by many college students.

Mikey had a few different duties there over the period of time that he was employed. During his sophomore year, he was offered the job of being one of their DJ's for the various events that they organized. Mikey was thrilled about this opportunity, since he loved music and the messages that songs could give. As a DJ, song selection was very important to him. He really worked hard to play what was popular, and also what was fun music for dancing. Mikey truly loved this job, and he loved the people he worked for there!

It did not take long for Mikey to become popular with other college students in his DJ role. His thick auburn hair that curled out from beneath his Minnesota Twins baseball cap, along with his darling smile, could melt anyone's heart. He was known as DJ "Mikey-Mo." And there was one song that he consistently played at every event. It was "Love Generation" by Bob Sinclar. "Love Generation" is about peace, love, and unity. He wanted everyone to be the love generation! This became Mikey's trademark song, and it was one that he played everywhere he went, no matter what he was doing. What a message he was trying to give to others his age!

Mikey talked to me about this song, wanting me to listen closely to the lyrics and grasp their deeper meaning.

They encourage peace and love to everyone we meet. We shouldn't worry about a thing, because everything will be all right. There is eternity. Mikey would say, "Isn't this awesome, Mom? This song is absolutely sweet!"

Mikey left this earth at the highest point of his life. He told his boss on the day before his passing that his life couldn't get any better. He was on top of the world and living the dream!

* * *

I had two vivid premonitions that Mikey was going to die at a young age, one of them just a few months before the accident. Mikey's dad had one as well, on the day we left Mikey in Colorado when we brought him down for his freshman year of college. I now feel it was our subconscious awareness of the plan. I also feel that we were being prepared for what was to come.

Mikey stayed out in Colorado during his summer break in 2007 because he wanted to continue his job as a DJ. He did come home to Minnesota to visit in July. When I first saw him, I noticed that he had a bad sunburn on his nose. I told him he needed to wear sunblock more. I said, "Melanoma has occurred in our family. I don't want you to get that deadly skin cancer."

Mikey looked at me and said, "Mom, something else is going to get me long before melanoma ever does!" This statement shocked me. He repeated it twice. After the accident in September of 2007, this comment quickly popped into my head. I felt he subconsciously knew that his time was coming.

I now realize what Mikey was trying to do before he left the earth. He was laying down a foundation for what was to come, and for his future role of teaching what is truly most important for us here in a way that his youthful peers on earth could understand and accept. It is all about love. He continues with that same message through the veil! Mikey tells me he really has no regrets. He lived his life here to the fullest. He does tell me that he was having fun, and he wishes he could have stayed here longer, but he needed to leave. His time here was up, and now he had work to do!

* * *

The physical loss of my precious son was absolutely devastating to me. Pain beyond pain. But from the very beginning, I knew in my heart someone I loved so much could not possibly be gone forever! I knew he couldn't be far away. Our family was just too close and connected. I opened my heart to what was happening around me. I never doubted the signs or dreams I received, no matter what others thought or said. I knew it was Mikey. And it is! He is as alive as ever, just in a different form and dimension, right next door! Always remember that we will see our loved ones again. The heavenly dimensions are truly all around us. They will continue to help us on our journey of life until we meet again. Then it will be time for one heck of a party!

My mission in going public with Mikey's story and messages about the afterlife is to give hope, peace, and comfort to others. Mikey asks that I share his messages about the importance of love and being positive in our ways while we are on earth.

We need to embrace and believe in the loving guidance that is unseen!

Glossary

Mikey uses some words and terms with specific meanings that may be unfamiliar to the reader. The definitions given here are entirely his own, delivered to his mother by pendulum.

Afterlife: The term interchanged with the word heaven. It is the many dimensions that exist all around us based on vibrations. It is our true home.

Angel Realms: The upper-level realms where Angels reside.

Angels: Loving helpers that are beings specifically dedicated to assisting others on earth and in other dimensions who help protect and guide. They do not come to earth to take on a general life plan like we do. These spiritual entities are pure in love. They may appear with or without wings.

Apports: An object that appears in your earthly dimension by the effort of us in the afterlife. Apports are energy-produced items brought to the earth dimension when we, in the afterlife, change the item's vibration. Altering the vibratory rate of an object can make it move into a different dimension. When something becomes compatible in its vibration to that of the earthly dimension, it can be seen and appear as solid. Basically, the object just shows up out of nowhere, or at least that is how it would seem to you on earth!

Archangels: Celestial spiritual entities of great ability and love. They can be involved in many roles of assistance to others, always in a positive and powerful way. They too will assist in different dimensions. They are the direct helpers of God.

Aspects: Word often used with dimensions. A vibrational variance or difference within the dimension.

Astral Travel/Realms: The dimensions in which astral travel happens are considered the communication and interactive realms for many. They are dimensions not considered to be in the true afterlife. However, much interaction can occur here with beings from many aspects and other dimensions.

The Beatitudes: Jesus said:

> "Blessed are the poor in spirit, for theirs is the Kingdom of Heaven.

Blessed are those who mourn, for they will be comforted.
Blessed are the meek, for they will inherit the earth.
Blessed are those who hunger and thirst for righteousness, for they will be filled.
Blessed are the merciful, for they will be shown mercy.
Blessed are the pure in heart, for they will see God.
Blessed are the peacemakers, for they will be called children of God.
Blessed are those who are persecuted because of righteousness, for theirs is the kingdom of Heaven.
Blessed are you when people insult you, persecute you and falsely say all kinds of evil against you because of me. Rejoice and be glad, because great is your reward in Heaven, for in the same way they persecuted the prophets who were before you."
{Matthew 5: 3–12, New International Version (NIV) Bible}

Channeling: A type of direct communication between a spiritual being in the afterlife and an individual on earth. It is telepathic in nature and can be fluent. This is how I communicate with my mom, along with using the pendulum with my energy.

Communication dreams: These are dream experiences that occur that are so real to you that you can feel, see, and hear your loved one who has passed over. They are very vivid and stay strong in your memory. This type of dream often occurs in the astral dimensions, which are higher than the vibratory rate of earth and very near the afterlife levels. You are literally meeting your loved one there. The silver cord allows the living to travel out of their physical bodies so this can happen.

Death: The process that occurs to release our true being (soul) from our physical body. The silver cord severs, resulting in death of our physical body. Our soul returns to the afterlife.

Dimensions: The infinite vibrational aspects of reality that exist everywhere and all around us.

Earth: A planet within a material realm or dimension, to which souls (or spiritual beings) choose to travel from the afterlife in order to take on a life in the physical human form. It is a place where individuals take on a general life plan with experiences to exercise and challenge their free will in various positive and negative situations. Earth is our school.

Earth-bounds: Souls that decline or refuse to cross over to the afterlife dimensions, even with guidance. They remain in the earthly dimension, even though they are free of their physical body.

Energy: Literally everyone and everything that exists in all the infinite dimensions is energy. There is a vibrational component to everything.

ET's or Extra-Terrestrials: These are beings from one dimension that travel to another dimension by altering their vibration. It is inter-dimensional travel. ET's are entities on a journey just like we are, and are part of the Source. Each of them belongs to a type of soul group as well.

Faith: The belief in something we cannot see as fact.

Ghosts: Another term used for earth-bounds.

God: A Unity of Absolute Pure Love which is Infinite. The Collective or Source of all that exists. We are all part of this Unity. The human mind cannot comprehend the true "concept" of God. God does not have a body, a gender, or any human failings. God is far greater than a bearded man sitting in a big chair on a throne.

Heaven: The term interchanged with the word afterlife. Heaven is the many dimensions that exist all around us based on vibrations. It is our true home.

Hell: Can be considered the two lowest planes or categories of the afterlife. These dimensions are dreary, not pleasant, and low in vibration. Understand that there is no eternal damnation. There is always loving guidance available if individuals want to improve themselves.

Higher self: It is the true essence of our being that resides in heaven. Our higher self holds all of our knowledge and understanding that we have gained through all of our experiences. Think of it as your suitcase of everything that you have learned being stored away until you return from your adventure. Then you will add more items to it from this last lifetime!

Hot tub: Everyone on earth needs to have one! They are the best!*

Human body: Our physical vehicle that we use while we are on earth to obtain our experiences here. It is temporary. Our true being or soul is eternal. We never end!

Love: A state of being, an emotion, thought, act, or feeling that always has a positive vibration to it. Positive vibrations are always higher in frequency. The higher your vibration, the more spiritually progressed you are. Love is truly what it is all about!

Love Generation: My favorite song while I was on earth, which was written by Bob Sinclar. As a DJ, this was the message I was trying to bring to you! Listen to the amazing lyrics. Be the love generation. Peace and love to everyone you meet!

Medium: An individual on earth that has the ability to communicate directly in some way with a spiritual being who has transitioned back to the afterlife.

NDE or Near Death Experience: An experience an individual has when they may be close to death, where they are traveling outside of their physical body. This travel may include a different dimension than earth with interactions with others who are in the afterlife dimensions. Our silver cord allows this to happen. These experiences are very vivid and feel very real to us. With a NDE, we always return to our physical body. Death of the body does not occur. It is not a true and complete transition to the afterlife because the silver cord remains intact. Therefore, the experience can represent what is real in the afterlife, or it may not.

Negative energy: Energy that has a low vibration and is low in love.

OBE or Out of Body Experience: An experience an individual can have when they travel outside of their physical body on earth to go to a different vibrational dimension. We can have interactions with others who are in the afterlife dimensions. Often these experiences occur in the astral realms. This can occur in a dream, or in a meditative or hypnotic state.

Orb: Spiritual energy of a loved one who has passed, which can sometimes be captured on a digital camera. It can appear as a round ball or orb of light in the picture. They can vary in color.

Passing Over: Our true being returns to the heavenly dimensions.

Planes: Word often used to define the categories of dimensions in heaven or the afterlife.

Positive energy: Energy that has a high vibration, where love is truly the basis.

Realm: Word often used, but meaning the same as dimension.

Reincarnation: A spiritual being choosing to come back to the earthly dimension to take on a general life plan in a physical human body and have experiences here.

Religion: an organized man-made institution with man-made rules that is established as a means of how to worship God.

Satan/devil: There is no one Satan or devil. There are negative energies and entities that are low in love.

Sign: A type of spiritual communication that is often used by loved ones who have passed over, where their energy is utilized to manipulate objects, small animals, certain types of insects, electrical items, etc, to let loved ones know they are all right and very much still alive.

Silver cord: The energy projection from our true spiritual being (soul) that connects us to our physical body on earth.

Sin: A word used by humans associated with certain acts that they have labeled as bad. It holds on to the influences of judgment. In the afterlife, all actions are based on vibration only. The more loving the action, the higher the vibration; the less loving the action, the lower the vibration. Spiritual growth comes from raising our vibration to a higher level.

Snowboarding: The sweetest winter sport on earth!

Soul: Word sometimes used to describe our true spiritual being, our consciousness, or mind.

Spirit guides: Generally more advanced souls that stay back in heaven and take on the role of guiding another soul/individual on earth to try to keep them on track with their general life plan and what they wanted to experience in this lifetime. Often they are in the same soul group of the individual they are guiding.

Spiritual being: An individual or soul that is free of a physical body.

Spiritual communication: Communication between an individual on earth and a spiritual being in another dimension. This can be done in a variety of ways.

Spiritual growth: Increasing our vibration of our true being by how we act and work through our many experiences on earth and in other dimensions. Having loving and positive ways progresses us spiritually.

Synchronicities: A series of events that occur on earth to individuals that are coordinated and guided by spiritual beings in the afterlife. Often these events lead to a specific goal that is desired by the spiritual beings. This goal can be for meeting someone specifically, or for getting a message across to that individual for future reference.

Transition: Word interchanged with passing over, crossing over, or death. Our true spiritual being (soul) leaves our physical body to move from the earthly dimension to a dimension in the afterlife.

*__RG's Note:__ Before Mikey's death, he had been petitioning his parents to install a hot tub. When I discovered that a sixth-level being had included yet one more plea for a hot tub in his glossary of spiritual terms, I laughed!

65172636R00097

Made in the USA
Lexington, KY
03 July 2017